Practical Security Autoi and Testing

Tools and techniques for automated security scanning and testing in DevSecOps

Tony Hsiang-Chih Hsu

BIRMINGHAM - MUMBAI

Practical Security Automation and Testing

Commissioning Editor: Karan Sadawana
Acquisition Editor: Heramb Bhavsar
Content Development Editor: Roshan Kumar
Technical Editor: Shweta Jadhav
Copy Editor: Safis Editing
Project Coordinator: Namrata Swetta
Proofreader: Safis Editing
Indexer: Priyanka Dhadke
Graphics: Alishon Mendonsa
Production Coordinator: Shraddha Falebhai

First published: January 2019

Production reference: 2310119

Published by Packt Publishing Ltd.
Livery Place
35 Livery Street
Birmingham
B3 2PB, UK.

ISBN 978-1-78980-202-3

www.packtpub.com

`mapt.io`

Mapt is an online digital library that gives you full access to over 5,000 books and videos, as well as industry leading tools to help you plan your personal development and advance your career. For more information, please visit our website.

Why subscribe?

- Spend less time learning and more time coding with practical eBooks and Videos from over 4,000 industry professionals

- Improve your learning with Skill Plans built especially for you

- Get a free eBook or video every month

- Mapt is fully searchable

- Copy and paste, print, and bookmark content

Packt.com

Did you know that Packt offers eBook versions of every book published, with PDF and ePub files available? You can upgrade to the eBook version at `www.packt.com` and as a print book customer, you are entitled to a discount on the eBook copy. Get in touch with us at `customercare@packtpub.com` for more details.

At `www.packt.com`, you can also read a collection of free technical articles, sign up for a range of free newsletters, and receive exclusive discounts and offers on Packt books and eBooks.

Contributors

About the author

Tony Hsiang-Chih Hsu is a senior security architect, software development manager, and project manager with more than 20 years' experience in security services technology. He has extensive experience of the **Secure Software Development Lifecycle (SSDLC)** in relation to activities including secure architecture/design review, secure code review, threat modeling, automated security testing, and cloud service inspection. He is also an in-house SDL trainer, having offered hands-on courses totaling in more than 300 hours. He is also the author of *Hands-on Security in DevOps*, and a co-author of several **Open Web Application Security Project (OWASP)** projects, including the OWASP testing guide, a proactive control guide, deserialization, cryptographic, and the XXE prevention cheatsheet.

About the reviewers

Anand Tiwari is an information security professional with nearly 5 years' experience in offensive security, with expertise in mobile, web application, and infrastructure security. He has authored an open source tool called Archery, and has presented at BlackHat, DEFCON, HITB, and ITEM conferences. His research primarily focuses on Android and iOS mobile applications. In his spare time, he writes code and experiments with open source information security tools.

Lawrence Liang serves as a cybersecurity solutions lead in a large public corporation. Prior to his current role, Lawrence assumed a variety of technical and managerial roles in several Fortune 500 companies focusing on IT infrastructure and security management for global clients. Lawrence earned his MBA from the University of Calgary, Canada, and his Bachelor of Software Engineering from Jinan University, China.

Packt is searching for authors like you

If you're interested in becoming an author for Packt, please visit `authors.packtpub.com` and apply today. We have worked with thousands of developers and tech professionals, just like you, to help them share their insight with the global tech community. You can make a general application, apply for a specific hot topic that we are recruiting an author for, or submit your own idea.

Table of Contents

Preface

This book is aimed at software developers, architects, testers, and QA engineers looking to build automated security testing frameworks alongside their existing **Continuous Integration (CI)** frameworks to achieve security quality in the software development and testing cycle.

It will teach you how to adopt security automation techniques to continuously improve your entire software development and security testing cycle. This book aims to combine security and automation to protect web and cloud services. This practical guide will teach you how to use open source tools and techniques to integrate security testing tools directly into your CI/**Continuous Delivery (CD)** framework. It will also show you how to implement security inspection at every layer, such as secure code inspection, fuzz testing, REST API testing, privacy testing, infrastructure security testing, and fuzz testing. With the help of practical examples, it will also teach you how to implement a combination of automation and security in DevOps. Furthermore, it will cover topics on the integration of security testing results so that you can gain an overview of the overall security status of your projects.

This book best fits those in the following roles and scenarios:

- Developers who are not familiar with secure coding rules, but need effective and automated secure code inspection with existing CI/CD integration.
- Development and QA teams who would like to perform security automation at different levels, such as the API, fuzz, functional, and infrastructure levels, but may have a gap to bridge in order to achieve automated security testing.
- Security team members who are finding that the testing output of their various security testing tools is not easily understood by non-security testing teams. In such cases, a universally recognizable security testing report is needed so that everyone can understand the overall security status of a project. (For these cases, behavior-driven and acceptance testing frameworks will be introduced.)

By the end of this book, you will be well versed in implementing automation security at all stages of your software development cycle, and will also have learned how to build your own in-house security automation platform for your cloud releases.

Who this book is for

This book is for anyone in any of the following positions:

- Software or operations managers who may need a security automation framework to apply to existing engineering practices
- Software developers who are looking for effective security tools, for automated code inspection for C/C++, Java, Python, and JavaScript
- Software testers who need security testing cases to be automated with both white-box/black-box tools such as API, fuzz, web, infrastructure and privacy security testing, with open source tools and script templates
- Software operations teams who need to perform automated software security scanning and an infrastructure configuration inspection before deployment to production.

What this book covers

Chapter 1, *The Scope and Challenges of Security Automation*, discusses the challenges of security automation and gives an overview of security automation tools and frameworks. The required skills, security tools, and automation frameworks will be introduced. This will help you to gain the foundational knowledge required for you to build security automation measures in the coming chapters. Finally, we will also set up some sample vulnerable source code, as well as an application, for practicing security scanning in the coming chapters. This will include an illustration of dynamic security testing techniques (OWASP ZAP, Nmap, and Fuzz) and static code inspection with automation frameworks (such as Selenium, Robot Framework, JMeter, and **behavior-driven development (BDD)**), as well as a detailed look at mobile security testing framework integration in several hands-on case studies.

Chapter 2, *Integrating Security and Automation*, introduces how security and automation can be integrated. Since both security testing and automation testing require domain expertise and very particular tools, this chapter will introduce how to bake automation into existing security testing frameworks to improve testing coverage and efficiency. We will also discuss how security testing practices and tools can be integrated into your in-house automation testing framework.

Chapter 3, *Secure Code Inspection*, discusses white-box testing techniques for the secure reviewing of code. For an in-house software development team, it's a challenge to review all the source code for every software release. This is not only due to the pressure of release cycles, but also due to the impracticality of requiring every developer to be familiar with all the secure coding best practices for all different programming languages, such as Java, C/C++, and Python. Therefore, we will demonstrate how to build your own automated secure coding platform with open source solutions for every release.

Chapter 4, *Sensitive information and Privacy Testing*, discusses how to use automated scanning to prevent the disclosure of sensitive information in every software release. There are three typical scenarios where this kind of thing can be applied. The first is where sensitive information is included in the source code, such as an include key, a hardcoded password, a hidden hotkey, an email address, or an IP or URL. Secondly, sensitive information can also be stored in cookies, since cookies can collect the browsing behaviors of users. Finally, large projects handling massive amounts of data require effective ways of identifying and protecting any **Personal Identifiable Information (PII)** stored in the database.

Chapter 5, *Security API and Fuzz Testing*, explores API and fuzz testing. As cloud software releases can be on an API-level basis, there can be hundreds of APIs released at a time. The software development team will definitely need an effective way to automate security testing for every API release. In this chapter, we use an online pet store case study to see how you can build your automated API security testing framework with various tools. API security testing focuses more on data injection and abnormal payloads. Therefore, fuzz testing will also be introduced as random data input and security injection for automated API security testing.

Chapter 6, *Web Application Security Testing*, is where we will use an online shopping site, Hackazon, to demonstrate how to achieve automated web security testing. The key challenge in automating web application testing is walking through the UI business flow while doing security inspection. Doing so requires not only security scanning capabilities but also web UI automation. We will be using security tools such as ZAP and web UI automation frameworks such as Selenium and Robot Framework. Using these tools can effectively improve your security testing coverage. We will share some tips and tools for making web automation easier.

Chapter 7, *Android Security Testing*, focuses on Android. It's a common practice to do a security check before an Android application release. However, doing so when releases can be so frequent and so many can be a real challenge. The automated security testing process for an Android mobile application requires submissions for APK binaries, reversing the APK for secure source code inspection, manifest configuration checks, and generating testing results – we'll be looking at all of this in this chapter. Besides that, we will also introduce mobile security-related practices, such as OWASP mobile security testing and Android secure coding practices.

Chapter 8, *Infrastructure Security*, will focus on infrastructure and platform security. For a **Platform-as-a-Service (PaaS)** or even for **Software-as-a-Service (SaaS)** providers, it's vital to ensure that the infrastructure is secure. Therefore, the security operations team will need to do regular scanning of the infrastructure to ensure security configurations for security compliance. Infrastructure security includes secure configuration with web services, security of databases and OSes, secure communication protocols such as TLS v1.2, and the use of secure versions of third-party components and dependencies. We will illustrate how to set up your own automated scanning framework to run these regular secure configuration inspections.

Chapter 9, *BDD Acceptance Security Testing*, will discuss the challenges of cross-team communication within large software development teams. For instance, the team who executed the security testing may understand the tests carried out and their results, but other non-technical teams such as product management and marketing may not gain the same understanding just from reading the testing reports. Therefore, we will introduce BDD acceptance testing with automated security testing. We will use security testing tools on top of BDD security automation testing frameworks and hook into the testing process.

Chapter 10, *Project Background and Automation Approach*, will introduce a project and the security objectives necessary for proceeding with automated security in the ensuing chapters. We will also explore what considerations need to be made when it comes to automation framework selection. For instance, some tools are good for specific security testing but may have shortcomings when it comes to automation framework integration. Finally, we will set up all the necessary environmental conditions for the coming security automation practices.

Chapter 11, *Automated Testing for a Web Application*, will use three case studies to teach you about different security automation techniques against the vulnerable NodeGoat site. The first case study looks at automating the OWASP ZAP by using the ZAP-CLI, which will help to identify initial security issues in a website before authentication. In the second case study, we will be using Selenium to identify security issues concerning user sign-in. In the final case, we will use JMeter for sign-in with external CSV data to detect potential command injection security issues.

Chapter 12, *Automated Fuzz API Security Testing*, looks at API Fuzz testing, which can be one of the most effective and efficient means of security and automation testing. API fuzz testing involves generating fuzz data as data input, sending HTTP requests with fuzz data, and analyzing the HTTP response for security issues. We will demonstrate several API fuzz automation tools (including Wfuzz and 0d1n), fuzz techniques, and integration with automation testing frameworks (such as Selenium and Robot Framework data-driven testing).

Chapter 13, *Automated Infrastructure Security*, will demonstrate how to automate infrastructure security testing against the NodeGoat website. The infrastructure security testing will include testing for known vulnerable JavaScript libraries, insecure SSL configurations, and advanced Nmap NSE script testing techniques for web security. At the end, we will also illustrate how to apply BDD automation frameworks to SSLScan and Nmap.

Chapter 14, *Managing and Presenting Testing Results*, covers how we consolidate and present security testing findings as a whole to stakeholders. Executing and managing several security testing projects at a time can be a challenge. The security team, the project team, and management would like to know the security status of each project. This requires the consolidation of the results from some previously mentioned security testing tools into one portal or summary document. We will need to not only manage all the security testing tools execution results, but also present them in a security dashboard that clearly displays the overall security posture of a project. We will introduce some approaches and tools to achieve this goal.

Chapter 15, *Summary of Automation Security Testing Tips*, summarizes the key security automation techniques and tips from all the previous chapters. This chapter can be used as a quick reference guide or as an overall review of security automation.

Appendix A, *List of Scripts and Tools*, summarizes the tools and commands used throughout all the chapters.

Appendix B, *Solutions*, includes all the answers, to the questions provided within the chapters.

To get the most out of this book

To get the most out of this book, you will need the sample code from the Packt Publishing GitHub repository. You will also need an Ubuntu virtual image, and you'll need to download the security testing tools and frameworks mentioned in the book.

Download the example code files

You can download the example code files for this book from your account at `www.packt.com`. If you purchased this book elsewhere, you can visit `www.packt.com/support` and register to have the files emailed directly to you.

You can download the code files by following these steps:

1. Log in or register at `www.packt.com`.
2. Select the **SUPPORT** tab.
3. Click on **Code Downloads & Errata**.
4. Enter the name of the book in the **Search** box and follow the onscreen instructions.

Once the file is downloaded, please make sure that you unzip or extract the folder using the latest version of:

- WinRAR/7-Zip for Windows
- Zipeg/iZip/UnRarX for Mac
- 7-Zip/PeaZip for Linux

The code bundle for the book is also hosted on GitHub at `https://github.com/PacktPublishing/Practical-Security-Automation-and-Testing`. In case there's an update to the code, it will be updated on the existing GitHub repository.

We also have other code bundles from our rich catalog of books and videos available at `https://github.com/PacktPublishing/`. Check them out!

Download the color images

We also provide a PDF file that has color images of the screenshots/diagrams used in this book. You can download it here: `http://www.packtpub.com/sites/default/files/downloads/9781789802023_ColorImages.pdf`.

Conventions used

There are a number of text conventions used throughout this book.

CodeInText: Indicates code words in text, database table names, folder names, filenames, file extensions, pathnames, dummy URLs, user input, and Twitter handles. Here is an example: "Mount the downloaded WebStorm-10*.dmg disk image file as another disk in your system."

A block of code is set as follows:

```
saxReader.setFeature("http://apache.org/xml/features/disallow-doctype-
decl", true);
saxReader.setFeature("http://xml.org/sax/features/external-general-entities
", false);
saxReader.setFeature("http://xml.org/sax/features/external-parameter-entiti
es", false);
```

Any command-line input or output is written as follows:

```
$ ag   -w   md5   d:\<targetPath>
```

Bold: Indicates a new term, an important word, or words that you see onscreen. For example, words in menus or dialog boxes appear in the text like this. Here is an example: "Select **System info** from the **Administration** panel."

Warnings or important notes appear like this.

Tips and tricks appear like this.

Get in touch

Feedback from our readers is always welcome.

General feedback: If you have questions about any aspect of this book, mention the book title in the subject of your message and email us at customercare@packtpub.com.

Errata: Although we have taken every care to ensure the accuracy of our content, mistakes do happen. If you have found a mistake in this book, we would be grateful if you would report this to us. Please visit www.packt.com/submit-errata, selecting your book, clicking on the Errata Submission Form link, and entering the details.

Piracy: If you come across any illegal copies of our works in any form on the Internet, we would be grateful if you would provide us with the location address or website name. Please contact us at copyright@packt.com with a link to the material.

If you are interested in becoming an author: If there is a topic that you have expertise in and you are interested in either writing or contributing to a book, please visit authors.packtpub.com.

Reviews

Please leave a review. Once you have read and used this book, why not leave a review on the site that you purchased it from? Potential readers can then see and use your unbiased opinion to make purchase decisions, we at Packt can understand what you think about our products, and our authors can see your feedback on their book. Thank you!

For more information about Packt, please visit packt.com.

The Scope and Challenges of Security Automation

1

This first chapter will discuss the challenges of security automation and take an overview of security automation tools and frameworks. The required skills, security tools, and automation frameworks will also be introduced. This will help you to gain the foundational knowledge required to build security automation measures in the coming chapters. Finally, we will also set up some sample vulnerable source code, as well as an application, for practicing security scanning in the coming chapters. This will include an illustration of dynamic security testing techniques (OWASP ZAP, NMAP, and fuzz) and static code inspection with automation frameworks (such as Selenium, Robot Framework, JMeter, and **behavior-driven development (BDD)**), as well as a look at mobile security testing framework integration in several hands-on case studies. In the later chapters, we will be using a project to apply all the security testing tools and automation frameworks discussed in this book.

We will explore the following topics in this chapter:

- The purposes and myths of security automation
- The required skills and suggestions for security automation
- General environment setup for coming labs

The purposes and myths of security automation

The purpose of security automation is to discover all potential security defects before any software release by applying both open source security tools and automation testing frameworks. However, security automation doesn't mean to completely replace manual security testing. Security automation aims to reduce the amount of repeated manual testing and increase testing coverage in an efficient manner. Potential security flaws can exist anywhere, from the source code and third-party components to an insecure configuration or vulnerable infrastructure. As the release cycles of cloud services and software development are getting shorter, the development team needs not only functional testing but also automated security testing. If your team is planning on implementing security automation, it's suggested that you begin with the following resources:

Resource on common security issues	How it could help
OWASP (Open Web Application Security Project) Top 10 Application Security Risks	This lists general web application security risks, such as injection, authentication, **XML external entity** (**XXE**) attacks, and misconfiguration. The OWASP also suggests related testing tools and prevention controls for each security issue.
CWE Top 25 Software Errors	This lists the most common software coding errors, such as SQL injection, **Cross-site request forgery** (**CSRF**), and buffer overflow. It can be a good checklist for a code-security review.

Security testing can be a tedious and repetitive process. The functional testing may only need to ensure the functionality, but the security testing needs to cover various kinds of the testing scenarios, such as authentication, authorization, XXE, injection, deserialization, and more (see the OWASP resource mentioned in the previous table). Therefore, a certain level of automation would be helpful, considering security testing's repetitive nature, scope, and importance. Be reminded that our goal is not to automate 100% of security testing cases, but to focus on those testing cases that are manually executed and repeated, and so can be done more efficiently by automation. By automating those repeated security testing cases, penetration testers can take time to exploit in-depth weaknesses and logic flaws or review security requirements (all of which can't be done by automation).

When it comes to security automation, there are some challenges and some myths. A lack of proper security or automation knowledge leads to some misunderstanding of security automation. Here are some general suggestions and clarification. We will explore more through the different hands-on case studies in the coming chapters.

Myth 1 – doesn't security testing require highly experienced pentesters?

Our first myth is that security testing requires highly experienced penetration testers and automation testing can't find serious issues.

If we can guide the automation properly, serious security issues can be identified. On the other hand, automated security testing can also result in false-positive issues that need further manual verification. However, there are certain kinds of security testing scenarios that would be ideal for automation; some of those are listed here:

- Detecting the use of banned functions, risky APIs, or weak encryption algorithms. Automated systems can do a good job of scanning code for security issues if we properly define the patterns we are looking for.
- Weak RESTful API authentication and authorization behaviors, such as bypassing authorization vulnerabilities.
- Data input validation may require massive amounts of random testing data input. This kinds of data input testing technique is also called fuzz testing which the prepared data and payload are dynamically generated for the test subject in an attempt to make it crash.
- Repeated UI walk-through, sign-in, sign-out, and form fill are good examples of where web UI automation is required.
- Insecure misconfiguration of software components, databases, or web services.
- Known third-party vulnerabilities.

Myth 2 – isn't it time-consuming to build an automation framework?

Our second myth is that it takes too much time to build an automation framework and that daily development changes may break the automation.

For a development team with mature security testing practices, the adoption of an automation framework such as BDD, **data-driven testing (DDT)**, or Selenium can help with seamless security integration and improve security testing coverage. Adding security testing cases based on these existing automation frameworks won't necessarily take lots of effort and time, so long as the right tools and integration approaches are selected.

For security automation relating to UI flow, daily development changes may or may not break certain UI automation testing cases. It depends on how the UI components are located by the automation testing program. As a general rule of thumb, so long as the UI components are located by the automation testing framework, UI layout changes won't impact the automation.

Myth 3 – there are no automation frameworks that are really feasible for security testing

Our third myth is that there is no single automation framework that can cover the variety of security testing cases.

Now, due to the variety of security testing scenarios, it's true that there is no one single automation framework that can cover all security testing cases. Depending on the security testing scenario, however, we can plan related automation approaches with proper integration of security testing tools and an automation framework. The following table shows examples of security testing scenarios with different automation approaches:

Automation approaches	Mapping to security testing scenarios	Automation tools/frameworks
White box	• Secure code inspection • Secure configuration inspection	• Secure code analysis with **Visual Code Grepper** (**VCG**)
API testing	• Web/RESTful API security testing • Data Input testing (also called parameterized testing or data-driven testing)	• Robot Framework's requests library • JMeter • FuzzDB • OWASP ZAP

Web UI automation	• Logging in with different users or wrong accounts • Logging users out for session management testing • Creating a new user account • Brute-forcing a user account login	• Robot Framework • Selenium • OWASP ZAP

Automating web UI operations doesn't necessarily take lots of implementation effort or require you to be an expert in Selenium scripts. The Selenium IDE extension will help you to generate automated scripts when you operate UI flows:

- **Kantu Selenium IDE**: This generates HTML-format scripts. It supports parameterized testing by CSV, takes screenshots of each step for visual review, and can be executed from the command line.
- **Katalon Recorder (Selenium IDE for Chrome/Firefox)**: The key advantage of Katalon is being able to generate various kinds of automation scripts, including Java, Python, Robot Framework, C#, and Ruby scripts. This makes Katalon very flexible for further integration with other tools. It can also support screenshots and DDT by importing CSV files.

The required skills and suggestions for security automation

Security team developers and automation testing developers require different skill sets. Naturally, the core skills of automation testing developers and pentesters are different. However, achieving security testing automation won't be too difficult for anyone, so long as the appropriate tools and frameworks are adopted to reduce the learning curve and ensure consistent delivery quality. For example, the adoption of web UI automation will help security testing to explore the blind side of the user flows. However, web UI automation and the adoption of the Selenium automation framework can be a big challenge for the security testing team. This issue can be solved with the help of proper automation testing tools, which will be introduced in the coming chapters.

The skills that penetration testers and automation testing developers have in common are as follows:

- Familiar with a programming language, such as Python, PHP, Java, or C/C++
- Familiar with Windows, Linux and **TCP/IP (Transmission Control Protocol/Internet Protocol**), and HTTP networking

Those were some similar skills; the following table lists some key differences:

Penetration testers	Automation testing developers
• Ability to identify software vulnerabilities by OWASP Top 10 security issues and practices • Familiar with **Secure Software Development Life cycle (SSLDC)** and security frameworks such as Spring Security and Shiro • Familiar with the use of OWASP ZAP, SQLmap, Nmap, Wireshark, and SSLtest	• Familiar with unit testing, APIs, and web UI automation testing frameworks such as Robot Framework, Selenium, WebDriver, and JMeter • Familiar with the defect cycle, issue tracking, and **continuous integration/continuous delivery (CI/CD)** frameworks • Familiar with BDD frameworks • Familiar with DDT frameworks

General environment setup for coming labs

For coming hands-on practices, it's suggested that you prepare the following tools for the system environment. Please also refer to the official website for the installation or quick start guide of every tool:

- Git: `https://git-scm.com/downloads`
- Python 2.7 (Python 3.4 may also work): `https://www.python.org/downloads/`
- PyCharm: `https://www.jetbrains.com/pycharm/download/`
- Vulnerable C/C++ and Java source code: `https://samate.nist.gov/SRD/testsuite.php#standalone`
- Insecure Bank APK: `https://github.com/dineshshetty/Android-InsecureBankv2/tree/master/InsecureBankv2/app`
- GoatDroid APK: `https://github.com/linkedin/qark/blob/master/qark/sampleApps/goatdroid/goatdroid.apk`

Summary

In this chapter, we discussed the objective of security automation: to reduce repeated manual testing and increase testing coverage in an efficient manner. The OWASP Top 10 list for web application security issues and the CWE Top 25 list for secure coding issues were suggested as resources.

We also discussed some misunderstandings of security automation, such as the need for highly skilled penetration testers, the time it takes to build automation frameworks, and the perceived limitations of automation testing's effectiveness. Security automation testing can even identify serious security defects, and won't require lots of implementation efforts, so long as the right security tools and automation frameworks are integrated properly.

Last but not least, we also discussed the skills of security developers and automation testing developers. The common ground required between these two roles includes only knowledge of networking, HTTP/HTTPS protocols, an operating system, and at least one programming language. The automation test developer may focus more on automation testing frameworks such as BDD, DDT, Selenium, unit testing, and so on. On the other hand, the security tester may focus on using security tools and techniques to identify security issues. In the coming chapters, we will demonstrate how security and automation can integrate properly to identify security issues in a more effective manner.

Questions

1. Which of the following provides a list of the most common software coding errors and can be a good checklist for the team to do code-security reviews?
    1. OWASP Top 10 Application Security risks
    2. CWE Top 25 Software Errors
    3. SDL
2. Which one of the following statements is true?
    1. Security automation testing can't identify serious security issues
    2. Elements of the UI flow, such as sign-in and sign-out, can't be done by automation security testing
    3. Web UI automation can be done by using Selenium IDE (Kantu or Katalon) to reduce implementation effort

3. Which of the following automation frameworks does not do web UI automation?
    1. Robot Framework
    2. Selenium
    3. VCG

4. Which of the following is not a required skill for an automation testing developer?
    1. Familiar with OWASP Top 10
    2. Familiar with Python and Java
    3. Understanding of Windows and Linux

5. Which one of the following is not an automation testing framework?
    1. Robot Framework
    2. Selenium
    3. SQLMap

Further reading

- **CWE Top 25**: https://cwe.mitre.org/data/index.html
- **OWASP Top 10**: https://www.owasp.org/index.php/Category:OWASP_Top_Ten_Project
- **Robot Framework**: http://robotframework.org/
- **Kantu Selenium IDE user manual**: https://a9t9.com/kantu/docs
- **Katalon Recorder**: https://www.katalong.com/resources-center/blog/katalong-automation-recorder/

2
Integrating Security and Automation

We looked at the scope and challenges of security automation in Chapter 1, *The Scope and Challenges of Security Automation*. In this chapter, we will introduce how security and automation can be integrated. Since both security testing and automation testing require domain expertise and very particular tools, this chapter will introduce how to bake automation into existing security testing frameworks to improve testing coverage and efficiency. We will also discuss how security testing practices and tools can be integrated into your in-house automation testing framework.

The following topics will briefly be discussed in this chapter:

- The domains of automation testing and security testing
- Automation frameworks and techniques
- Automating existing security testing
- Security testing with an existing automation framework

The domains of automation testing and security testing

The domain of automation includes white-box code inspection, unit testing, acceptance testing, integration testing, API testing, and end-to-end UI testing. In terms of implementation effort, unit testing and white-box inspection usually take the least effort, while UI testing often takes the most effort, particularly in order to understand the UI business flow.

Therefore, most automated testing cases are done with unit testing or API-level testing. Automated UI testing may only cover the scenarios from a user perspective while the API testing may cover more business logic or exception handling use cases. The following diagram illustrates the different levels of automation testing and how much effort they take.

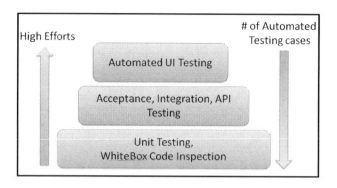

Levels of Automation Testing

On the other hand, the domain of security testing can be much broader. The following table lists the practices that come under the general umbrella of security testing. In this book, we will have some case studies to cover some of the topics in bold:

• **Information gathering** • **Vulnerability analysis** • Wireless attacks • **Web application exploitation tools** • Forensics tools • Stress testing • Sniffing and spoofing • **Password attacks** • **Maintaining access**	• Reverse engineering • **Reporting tools** • Hardware hacking • **Authentication** • **Authorization** • **Configuration management** • **Cryptography** • **Data validation**	• Denial of service • **Encryption** • Error handling • **Information disclosure** • Race conditions • **Session management** • **Secure transmission**

Automation frameworks and techniques

In this section, we will introduce some common automation testing frameworks, covering API, functional, UI, and mobile testing. Understanding the key characteristics of each automation framework will help the security team know how to integrate security testing and figure out what can be improved by automation.

UI functional testing for web, mobile, and windows

UI functional testing looks at the end user's perspective. It walks through the UI flow and verifies the response from the GUI. There are three testing target platforms: web services, mobile applications, and Windows applications. The following table lists some common open source/free automation frameworks:

Automation framework	Macaca	AutoIT	Selenium	Appium	Sikuli
Target	Mobile (iOS and Android) Web UI	Windows applications	Web UI	Mobile (iOS and Android)	Image-based Visual Testing
Programming language	Java, Python, and Node.js	BASIC-like script	Java, Python, C#, and Ruby	Java and Python	Visual images and BASIC-like script
Record and replay	UI Recorder	AutoIT Recorder	Selenium IDE	Desktop Inspector	Yes

HTTP API testing

UI testing may be prone to errors due to the instability of GUI responses. Another approach to functional testing that avoids the GUI is API-level testing. Since most web services provide RESTful APIs, API testing can be one of the most effective and efficient ways of automation testing.

Here are some common approaches to API testing techniques:

API testing tools	Java Rest-Assured	Python Requests	JMeter	Fiddler	Postman
Programming language	Java	Python	No	JavaScript-like Syntax	No
Record and replay	No	No	Yes	Yes	Yes
Verification (Assertion)	Java TestNG or JUnit	PyUnit	Yes	Yes	Yes
Proxy mode	No	No	Yes	Yes	Yes

For HTTP testing, the support of proxy mode gives the following benefit:

- Monitor HTTP request/response history
- Record and replay or modify specific HTTP requests
- Mock certain HTTP responses to reduce web server dependencies
- Simulate HTTP-based API testing as a mock web service.

HTTP mock server

The mock server works as a proxy between the testing client and target web services. For HTTP service testing, the mock server proxy can help test API interfaces to reduce the dependency or the readiness of the whole backend web services. It allows us to prepare client-side automation without the need to have the whole backend web services. When it comes to security testing, proxy mode helps to monitor HTTP traffic, send security payloads with HTTP requests, and analyze HTTP responses for potential security issues. Most web security scanners can run in proxy mode, including OWASP ZAP and Arachni.

Here are some of common free/open source mock server frameworks:

HTTP mock server	Key characteristics
Moco	If you just want to have a simple HTTP mock server with a few defined HTTP responses, Moco is highly recommended due to the ease of deployment and use. Moco is a standalone JAR and the HTTP response behaviors can be defined by one JSON configuration file. https://github.com/dreamhead/moco
mitmproxy	For an open source HTTPS proxy solution, mitmproxy is also highly recommended. The web interface makes it easy to use, just like Chrome Developer Tools. mitmproxy is a free and open source interactive HTTPS proxy. It provides a command line, web interface, and Python API to intercept, inspect, modify, and replay web traffic for both HTTP and HTTPS. https://mitmproxy.org/#mitmweb
GoReplay	GoReplay can capture and replay web traffic like TCPDump. It simply captures web traffic based on a given communication port. https://goreplay.org/

 Most of the web security testing tools are running as a web proxy. It's also called as **MITM (Man in The Middle)**. The Web Proxy will monitor the web traffic, and analyze the every responses to identify potential web security issues.

White-box search with GREP-like tools

There may be scenarios where we need to search specific patterns or keywords to identify potential issues. The GREP tool in Linux is a common search tool for source code or plain text configurations. For code-security reviews, here are some security scanning tools that provide GREP-like search functionality:

Search tools	Key characteristics
Code Review Audit Script Scanner	This is a one-shell script that includes all common code security issue patterns. No other dependency is required to run the script. `https://github.com/floyd-fuh/crass/blob/master/grep-it.sh`
Grep Rough Audit	This is a shell script that will read signatures for potential security issues in source code `https://github.com/wireghoul/graudit/`
GrepBugs	This scans security issues based on defined regular expression patterns `https://grepbugs.com/browse`
VisualCodeGrepper	This is a Windows scanner tool with defined regular expression security patterns `https://github.com/nccgroup/VCG`
Flawfinder	This is a simple C/C++ security source code scanner `http://www.dwheeler.com/flawfinder/`
ripgrep recursively searches	This is a powerful regular expression searcher `https://github.com/BurntSushi/ripgrep`

Behavior-driven development testing frameworks

Behavior-driven development (BDD) testing frameworks define the testing script in the format of "*Given...When...Then.*" Here is a typical example.

```
Given NMAP is installed
When I launch an NMAP network scan "nmap -F host"
Then the output should match "25 tcp open"
```

Here are some common BDD frameworks:

BDD framework	Usage and scenarios
Robot Framework	This is a common keyword-driven testing acceptance automation framework. Robot Framework is programming language independent, though Robot Framework itself was built by Python. `http://robotframework.org`
Behave	This is a Python-based BDD framework `https://github.com/behave/behave`
Jgiven	This is a Java-based BDD framework `http://jgiven.org/`
Gauntlt	It's a security testing BDD Framework. `http://gauntlt.org/`

In the comping chapters, we will demostrate the uses of Robot Framework and Gauntlt to achieve the security automation testing.

Testing data generators

For some testing scenarios, we may need to update the SQL database with testing data (such as names, phone numbers, IPs, email addresses, city names, and filenames), or to allow the web service to respond with basic sample data. Here are some tools that can generate testing data based on the user-defined data type or format such as (date, address, ID, numeric data or strings):

Tools	Usage and scenarios
Mockaroo	This provides an online data generator service that provides test data in CSV, JSON, and SQL formats, based on your defined data type `https://mockaroo.com/`
JSON Schema Faker	This generates JSON data based on a defined JSON schema `http://json-schema-faker.js.org/`
JS Faker	This provides a **command-line interface** (**CLI**) to generate the data type based on your options, such as system, name, address, and phone. It can also output based on the specified locale language. `https://github.com/lestoni/faker-cli`

Automating existing security testing

If the team already have certain security testing measures in place and would like to apply an automation testing framework to improve efficiency or reduce manual execution efforts, there are some recommended automation frameworks the team may consider. The following table details the automation frameworks that may help in various kinds of security testing scenarios:

Types of automation frameworks	The scenarios where the automation framework can help
Web UI automation (Selenium or Robot Framework)	• User registration flow • Authentication/authorization flow • Shopping cart and order payment flow • Forget password flow • PII (Personally identifiable information) -sensitive operations, such as profile update
API testing (JMeter)	• RESTful API testing with injection payloads
BDD testing Robot Framework or gauntlt	• When a BDD framework is applied to security testing, the purpose is to enhance cross-team communication and enable a non-security team to understand how security is tested
Fuzz Testing	• Security payload testing with various injection and buffer overflow testing
Data-driven testing (DDT)	• DDT testing is normally done with fuzz testing • DDT is normally included in the unit testing framework of the programming language

Security testing with an existing automation framework

If the team has done some automation testing, security testing can be built on top of it. For security testing to be integrated with automation frameworks, we need to consider the input data for the tool, the support of the API or CLI to trigger the execution, and the preferred testing report format, such as JSON, XML, or CSV. In addition, in order to consolidate all the testing reports generated by various security testing tools, we will introduce OWASP DefectDojo to import all the security findings and the security dashboard presentation. Therefore, the output format of the security testing tools is also part of the security testing tool selection criteria.

The following table lists some recommended security testing tools that provide flexible interfaces for automation framework integration, and the output formats can be imported into OWASP DefectDojo:

Type of security testing	Recommended tools for automation and rationale
Web security	**Arachni and OWASP ZAP**: Arachni provides both a CLI and a Ruby library that can help to achieve automation integration. OWASP ZAP provides a CLI, REST API, and other programming libraries for further integration.
Known vulnerable components	**OWASP Dependency Check**: This mainly scans for Java and .NET known vulnerable components **OpenVAS**: This scans for all known CVEs (Common Vulnerabilities and Exposures) for all system components **RetireJS**: This scans for vulnerable JavaScript libraries
Fuzz testing	**Radamsa**: This can dynamically generate fuzz data based on a given sample **SecLists and FuzzDB**: These are fuzz data sources that define common payloads for security testing
Networking	**Nmap**: The tool can be used to network communication ports, to identify the OS and services, and also to do vulnerability scan the whole infrastructure.
SSL (Secure Sockets Layer)	**SSLLabs-Scan and SSLyze**: These are common security scanners for misconfiguration of SSL/TLS (Transport Layer Security)
Secure code review	**Visual Code Grepper** (**VCG**): It's a Windows based secure code scan tool for general programming languages. **Grep Rough Audit:** It searches secure code issues based on regular expression patterns. **Bandit: It's Python secure code scan tool.**
Secure configuration	OpenSCAP Workbench provides GUI and security profiles for scanning common Linux OS configurations

Summary

This chapter introduces the integration of security and automation. The domain of automation testing covers white-box code inspection, unit testing, API testing, integration testing, and end-to-end UI integration testing. The automation technique being used may depend on the effort required and the automation rate. The security testing domain was also explored in this chapter. We will primarily be focused on common security issues for web applications and mobile applications, such as password attacks, data validation, information disclosure, session management, and secure transmission.

We also illustrated some security testing scenarios where automation frameworks can help. For example, the Selenium Web UI framework is used to walk through the UI flow for security tools to inspect security issues. JMeter can be used with security payloads to do RESTful API security testing. Robot Framework can integrate with ZAP to introduce BDD testing into the security testing cycle.

We also recommended some common open source security tools that provide either a CLI or a RESTful API interface for automation framework integration. These dealt with web security (Arachni and OWASP ZAP), known vulnerable components (RetireJS and OpenVAS), fuzz testing (SecLists and FuzzDB), networking (Nmap), SSL (SSLyze), secure code review (VCG), and OpenSCAP for OS secure configuration checks.

In the coming chapter, we will introduce white-box secure code review techniques and tools for common programming languages.

Questions

1. Which one of these is not part of security testing domain?
    1. BDD
    2. Information gathering
    3. Data validation
    4. Cryptography

2. Which one of the following is not used for UI functional testing?
    1. AutoIT
    2. Selenium
    3. Appium
    4. ZAP

3. Which of the following is used for HTTP API testing?
    1. JMeter
    2. Fiddler
    3. Python requests
    4. All of the above

4. Which of these is not the purpose of using a mock server?
    1. Reducing the dependencies of the backend web services
    2. Defining standard HTTP responses
    3. Doing UI functional testing
    4. Responding to the HTTP requests

5. Which of these is used for known vulnerabilities scanning?
    1. OpenVAS
    2. OWASP Dependency Check
    3. RetireJS
    4. All of above

Further reading

- **Arachni Scanner**: http://www.arachni-scanner.com/
- **OWASP ZAP**: https://www.owasp.org/index.php/OWASP_Zed_Attack_Proxy_Project
- **OWASP Dependency Check**: https://www.owasp.org/index.php/OWASP_Dependency_Check
- **OpenVAS**: http://www.openvas.org/
- **RetireJS**: https://retirejs.github.io/retire.js/
- **SecLists**: https://github.com/danielmiessler/SecLists
- **Nmap**: https://nmap.org/
- **ssllabs-scan**: https://github.com/ssllabs/ssllabs-scan
- **VCG**: https://github.com/nccgroup/VCG/tree/master/VCG-Setup/Release
- **Automated security testing for REST APIs**: https://github.com/flipkart-incubator/Astra
- **WireMock**: http://wiremock.org/
- **MockJS**: http://mockjs.com/examples.html
- **MockBin**: https://github.com/Kong/mockbin
- **PACT Python**: https://github.com/pact-foundation/pact-python/

- **Power Mock**: https://github.com/powermock/powermock
- **Mock-Server**: http://www.mock-server.com/#why-use-mockserver
- **WireMock**: https://github.com/tomakehurst/wiremock
- **Faker JS documentation**: http://marak.github.io/faker.js/
- **Faker JS source**: https://github.com/marak/faker.js/
- **Faker-CLI**: https://github.com/lestoni/faker-cli
- **JSON Schema Faker Source**: https://github.com/json-schema-faker/json-schema-faker

3
Secure Code Inspection

In this chapter, we will discuss white-box testing techniques for secure code review. For an in-house software development team, it's a challenge to review all the source code for every software release. This is not only because of the pressure of release cycles, but because of the impracticality of requiring every developer to be familiar with all the secure coding best practices for all different programming languages, such as Java, C/C++, and Python. Therefore, we will demonstrate how to build your own automated secure coding platform with open source solutions for every release.

This chapter will cover the following topics:

- Case study—automating a secure code review
- Secure coding best practices and methodology
- Vulnerable code patterns for every programming language
- Automating secure code scanning tools with Jenkins (using C/C++, Java, Python, JavaScript, and PHP)

Case study – automating a secure code review

Software Company-X releases cloud services. The Android development team in company-X is using IDE developer tools to do secure code review for released Android applications. However, the uses of the IDE developer tools may have less visibility of the whole project security status. The development manager is also looking for a secure coding inspection service that can establish consistent secure coding quality across projects. Therefore, a secure coding scanning service will be in a need.

Secure coding scanning service – SWAMP

The following diagram shows an ideal secure coding inspection service. It provides users or developers with interfaces to submit the source code or package. The interface for the operations could be a GUI, a RESTful API, **command-line interface (CLI)**, or a Jenkins plugin. The programming language that is supported varies from project to project, but common programming languages include Java, Android app, C/C++, and also web script languages such as PHP, Python, JavaScript, and Ruby. Once the coding scanning is done, the service is expected to deliver a comprehensive inspection report that identifies the vulnerability and offers remedial suggestions:

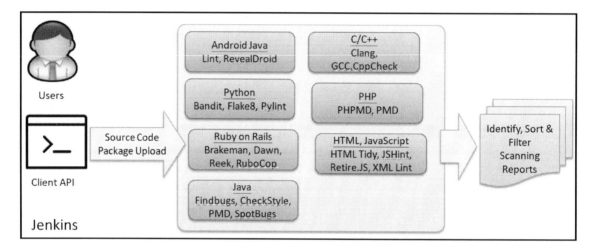

Secure code inspection framework

The **Software Assurance Marketplace (SWAMP)** provides a standalone software application called **SWAMP in a Box (SiB)**, which allows you to build your in-house secure code inspection services with the support of various scanning tools. SiB can be downloaded from here: `https://github.com/mirswamp/deployment`.

To demonstrate how the SWAMP works, we may clone or download the vulnerable Python API project as a ZIP package here: `https://github.com/rahulunair/vulnerable-api`. The SWAMP also provides the cloud service for the scanning service; just sign into the SWAMP portal by using your GitHub or Google accounts: `https://www.mir-swamp.org/`.

Step 1 – adding a new package

Once you have logged in to the SWAMP portal, create a new package by clicking **Packages** and then **Add New Packages**. Fill in the information as in the following screenshot. The package must be compressed into a ZIP archive to be uploaded to the SWAMP. In our example, we give `Bad Python` in the **Name** field, and select the previously downloaded ZAP, `vulnerable-api-mater.zip`:

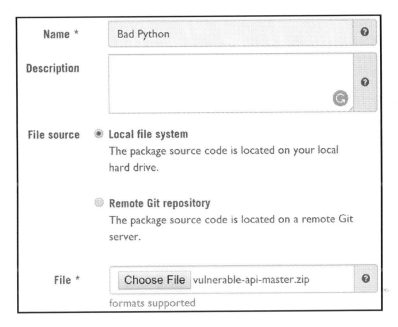

Project import in SWAMP

If it's uploaded correctly, the next step will require certain project information, such as source code and build information. We may keep the Python version as `Python2` and click **Next** for the next page to **Save New Package** at the end of the step.

Step 2 – running the assessment

Once the package is created, click the **Run New Assessment** button, then click **Save and Run** on the next page:

Assessments in SWAMP

Step 3 – viewing the results

When the assessment is done, you will be able to see the assessment results here: `https://www.mir-swamp.org/#results`. Or, you can navigate to **Home** then **Results**:

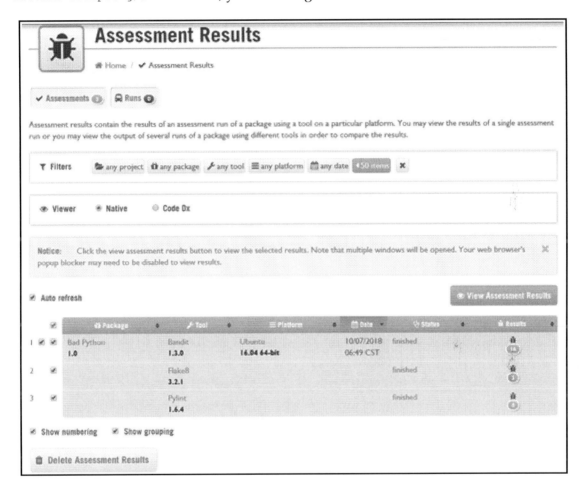

Assessments results in SWAMP

Take the vulnerable Python as an example: the SWAMP applies three scanning tools, Bandit, Flake8, and Pylint, for the scanning. We may review one of the scanning results by selecting the checkbox in front of the package name and clicking **View Assessment Results** button. This brings us to the options of **Native** or **Code Dx** view. The **Native** view provides a summary table of the identified security code issues, and the **Code Dx** view is an interactive interface with the original source code.

The following diagram shows a sample of the **Native** view:

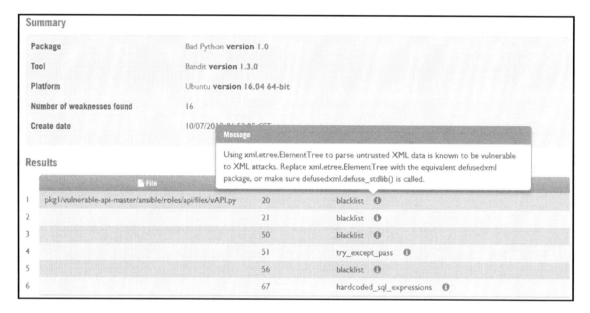

Message of results in SWAMP

Secure coding patterns for inspection

To perform a secure code scan, we must define the scanning rules based on common security issues and the programming language in question. It's fundamental to use keyword-driven expressions, regular expressions, or string operations for the scanning rules. The following table shows common risky APIs which may introduce security vulnerabilities and secure coding patterns which are indicators for potential security issues for various programming languages.

The **false positive** column indicates whether the search result requires further manual verification. For example, `Low` means that once the keyword is matched in the source code, the security issue can be confirmed without the need for further verification. `Med` means the identified patterns still require further verification:

Programming language	Risky API or insecure code patterns		False positive
General	Weak encryption	`Blowfish	DES	3DES	RC4	MD5	SHA1	XOR	ARC4	IDEA	ECB	CBC	TLS 1.0	SSL 2.0	Base64	RIPEMD	base64`	Low
	Insecure protocol	`SSL	HTTP	FTP	Telnet`	Low
	Hardcoded information	`Password	IP address	Email	Special Hotkey	URL	Mobile Number	Name`	High
C/C++	Command injection	`execl	execlp	execle	system	popen	WinExec	ShellExecute	execv	execvp	`	Med
	Buffer overflow	`fscanf|sscanf|vsscanf|vfscanf|scanf|vscanf|wscanf| sprintf|vsprintf|swprintf|vswprintf|snprintf|vsnprintf getchar|read|_gettc|fgetc|getc| memcpy|CopyMemory|bcopy|memmove lstrcpy|wcscpy|lstrcpyn|wcsncpy|_tcscpy|_mbscpy |strncat|strncpy`	Med
Java	Injection	`Runtime	ProcessBuilder	CommandLine	zookeeper.Shell	System.out.printf	createStatement`	Low
	Path traversal	`getAbsolutePath`	Low
	Deserialization	`XMLDecoder	xstream	readObject	readResolve	InvocationHandle	ObjectInputStream`	Med
	Weak random	`Java.util.Random`	Low
	URL injection	`url=	href=`	Low
	XML external entity (XXE)	`DocumentBuilder	XMLInputFactory	SAXReader	SAXParser	SAXBuilder	XMLReader	DocumentHelper	XMLInputFactory	XMLStreamReader`	Med
	URL authorization bypass	`.getRequestURL(	.getRequestURI`	Med
	File-handling validation	`ZipiInputStream	.endsWith(`	Med
	ZIP of Death	`ZipFile	ZipInputStream`	Med
	Information leakage	`FileNotFoundException	JARException	MissingResourceException	acl.NotOwnerException	ConcurrentException	ModificaitonException	InsufficientResourceException	BindException	OutOfMemoryError	StackOverflowException	SQLException`	Med
Python	Injection	`execfile	input	commands	subprocess`	Med
	Risky API	`pickle.load	eval`	Med

PHP	Injection	shell_exec | system | exec | popen | passthru | proc_open | pcntl_exec | eval | assert | preg_replace | create_function | preg_match | str_replace	Low
JavaScript	Risky API	eval | execScript | sessionStorage | localStorage	Low

This table uses the keywords and regular expression patterns approach to identifying security vulnerabilities in the source code. However, this kind of approach may have certain limitations. Some of the security issues may require further source code correlations to be identified. For advanced searches that go beyond the use of a regular expressions search in the source code, the open source ReBulk Python library can be considered. The ReBulk library allows developers to build more complex match rules to search for specific coding issues.

Quick and simple secure code scanning tools

We may identify secure code vulnerabilities by using the keywords, secure code patterns and risky APIs listed in the table in the previous section. This can be a simple and quick solution to apply to any partial source code. However, the biggest problem of this approach is the false-positive rate, which needs to be optimized by defining proper secure code regular expression match patterns. We will introduce two tools that can do a quick scan of the source code, based on key secure code patterns.

Automatic secure code inspection script in Linux

For this approach, we recommend an all-in-one shell script, the **Code Review Audit Script Scanner** (**CRASS**). This one script includes everything needed for secure code scanning, and it defines the secure code scanning patterns for Java, JSP, Flex Flash, .NET, PHP, HTML, Android, iOS, Python, Ruby, and C. It can easily be extended by editing the grep-it.sh file. We may use the same vulnerable Python project from before as our example for the following steps.

Step 1 – downloading the CRASS

Download the `grep-it.sh` script from
here: **https://github.com/floyd-fuh/crass/blob/master/grep-it.sh** , under the target
project folder. For example, we may download it under the `/vulpython` folder.

Alternatively, if you are using Git, execute the following command to download the script:

```
git    clone    https://github.com/floyd-fuh/crass/blob/master/grep-it.sh
```

Step 2 – executing the code review audit scan

Execute the command with a parameter to specify the target project folder. The following
command will scan the vulnerable source code under the `/vulpython` folder:

```
$ bash   grep-it.sh   ./vulpython
```

Step 3 – reviewing the results

Once the scanning is done, the scanning results will be output under the `\grep-output` folder of the target scanning project.

The scanning results will be generated into files separated by security topic, as shown in the
following diagram:

```
osboxes@osboxes:~/vulpython/grep-output$ ls
2_cryptocred_credentials_narrow.txt    4_general_exec_wide.txt
2_dotnet_unsafe_declaration.txt        4_general_hidden.txt
2_general_hacking_techniques_csrf.txt  4_general_https_urls.txt
3_cryptocred_ciphers_des.txt           4_general_http_urls.txt
3_cryptocred_ciphers_sha512.txt        4_general_popen_wide.txt
3_cryptocred_credentials_wide.txt      4_general_session_timeout.txt
3_cryptocred_password.txt              4_general_sql_cursor.txt
3_general_ip-addresses.txt             4_general_sql_sqlite.txt
3_general_popen_narrow.txt             4_java_string_comparison3.txt
3_general_schema.txt                   4_php_type_unsafe_comparison.txt
3_general_sqli_generic.txt             5_cryptocred_hash.txt
3_general_sql_insert.txt               5_cryptocred_hexdigest.txt
3_general_sql_select.txt               5_general_update.txt
3_java_sql_execute.txt                 5_html_autocomplete.txt
3_modsecurity_block.txt                5_java_strings.txt
4_general_base64_content.txt           5_python_is_object_identity_operator_general.txt
4_general_base64_urlsafe.txt
```

Code scan results

Automatic secure code inspection tools for Windows

This approach is very easy to deploy without the need to install other dependencies, and it doesn't require a whole buildable source code package to do the code scanning. For some cases, to identify security code issues, it requires not only to identify the risky API but also to review the context of the usage, which will be explained more in the next section.

For Windows users, the secure code scanning tool **Visual Code Grepper** (**VCG**) is recommended. It provides not only GUI but also CLI mode. It supports multiple programming languages, including C/C++, Java, PHP, VB, and C#. The default installation comes with details on the predefined banned and risky functions of each programming language in the configuration files (`*.conf`), and the rules can also be easily customized by editing the configuration files. Here are the steps to scan the project.

Step – downloading VCG (Visual Code Grepper)

Download the setup package and run the setup to install VCG on Windows. The installer is available here: `https://github.com/nccgroup/VCG/tree/master/VCG-Setup/Release`.

Step 2: Executing VCG

Executing `VisualCodeGrepper.exe` will directly launch VCG in GUI mode.

If you would like to execute in console mode, use the following command:

```
$ VisualCodeGrepper   -c  -v  -t   <DirectoryName>
```

For other options, please refer to the `Readme.txt` file in the URL below.

`https://github.com/nccgroup/VCG/blob/master/VCG-Setup/Release/README.txt`

Step 3: Reviewing the VCG scanning results

By default, the scanning results will be generated as `test1.csv` under the installed path. Alternatively, you may also use the **VCG GUI | File | Import Results from CSV File | `test1.csv`** to review the results with highlighted colors.

Case study – XXE security

The XXE security issue is one of the OWASP Top 10 security issues. The solution to the XXE issue is to disable XXE and **DTD (Document Type Definition)** processing. Therefore, when we are doing source code review, we are looking for whether the configuration of DTD is missing in the source code, as shown in the following example:

```
Factory.setFeature("http://apache.org/xml/features/disallow-doctype-decl",
true);
```

White-box review is still the most efficient approach to identifying XXE issues. The easiest thing to do is to discover whether one of the following XML libraries is being used to parse XML. We may use one of the tools such as CRASS or VCG mentioned in previous section to do such a search with the keywords listed here:

Programming language	Source code patterns for potential XXE issues
Java	SAXParser | SAXParserFactory | DocumentBuilderFactory | TransformerFactory | XMLReader | DOMParser | SAXBuilder | SAXReader | XMLInputFactory | SchemaFactory | DocumentBuilderFactoryImpl | DocumentBuilderImpl | SAXParserFactoryImpl | SAXParserImpl
C/C++	xmlCtxtRead | xmlCtxtUseOptions | xmlParseInNodeContext | xmlReadDoc | xmlReadFd | xmlReadFile | xmlReadIO | xmlReadMemory

Once these XML parser APIs are found in the source code, we will do a further manual review to check if the DTD resolution is explicitly disabled in the source code. Just be aware that to disable the DTD, it needs to be defined explicitly in the source. Take SAXreader as an example, to prevent XXE effectively, the following three lines are necessary.

```
saxReader.setFeature("http://apache.org/xml/features/disallow-doctype-
decl", true);
saxReader.setFeature("http://xml.org/sax/features/external-general-entities
", false);
saxReader.setFeature("http://xml.org/sax/features/external-parameter-entiti
es", false);
```

Although source code scanning can't do a perfect job in identifying the XXE issue, we still can use the techniques to narrow the scope in identifying the XXE issue.

Please also refer to OWASP XML Prevent CheatSheet for details. `https://www.owasp.org/index.php/XML_External_Entity_(XXE)_Prevention_Cheat_Sheet`

Case study – deserialization security issue

The deserialization security issue is commonly seen in Java, and is a **Remote Code Execution (RCE)** attack. Serialization is the process in Java of converting the state of an object into a byte stream (serialized object), which can be stored in files, memory, or a database. Deserialization is the reverse process, creating an object based on the byte stream.

For the deserialization attack, the serialized object becomes one of untrusted data input for the receiver to do the deserialization. The attack may tamper with or replace the serialized object with malicious code. This can be referred to in *CWE-502: Deserialization of untrusted data* `http://cwe.mitre.org/data/definitions/502.html`

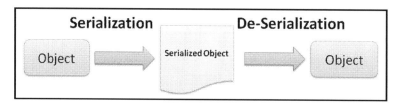

Process of deserialization

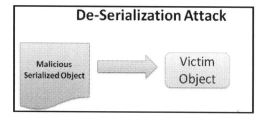

Deserialization attack

The serialized object can be stored or transmitted by memory, files, and networks. The hacker may tamper with the serialized object or inject malicious code so that the reader/receiver of the serialized object will be vulnerable to injection attacks:

To discern whether our Java project is vulnerable to the deserialization security issue, we can look for specific deserialization behaviors with API keywords. Although we can't completely automate code scanning here, we can at least narrow the scope of the review area:

Programming language	Source code patterns for potential deserialization security issues
Java	`XMLDecoder	XStream	readResolve	readExternal	ObjectInputSteam	readObject	readObjectNoData	java.lang.reflect.InvocationHandler	MethodHandler.invoke	Object.finalize |`

If none of the APIs listed here have been used, we don't need to worry much about the deserialization security issue. However, if one of APIs has been used in the source code, then it warrants further investigation; one of the following mitigations can be implemented:

- Whitelisting or blacklisting the deserialized class
- Adoption of any look-ahead Java deserialization library, such as `SerialKiller`

> To identify the security risks for injection attacks, it is suggested to clearly define what kinds of injection we are focused on. For example, the injection attacks may be categoritzed as SQL injection, Command injection, XSS, XXE, and so on. For a large scale project, try to focus on one type of injection at a time. This approach not only narrows the scope of the scan but also help to reduce false positives.

Summary

In this chapter, we introduced how to build your own secure code inspection system with the SWAMP. The SWAMP allows developers to submit their source code or package for automatic secure code review, helping them to identify critical security issues at the source-code level. The SWAMP provides cloud and on-premises versions. We demonstrated the steps for submitting a vulnerable Python project for a security review on SWAMP.

As we continue to look at secure code review, there are key security issues that we will focus on, such as weak encryption algorithms, insecure protocol, hardcoded sensitive information, and risky APIs that may result in command injection or buffer overflow. The list of risky APIs can be a reference to use when implementing a secure code review tool. In a case study of this chapter, we demonstrated the use of CRASS to scan vulnerable Python APIs. Furthermore, we also introduced another generic general secure coding inspection tool, VCG.

We discussed two security cases, the XXE and deserialization security issues. Once we are familiar with the security code patterns for identifying such security issues, we may use code inspection tools, such as CRASS and VCG, to identify the vulnerability in the source code.

In the coming chapter, we will apply similar code inspection techniques to look for sensitive information leakage and privacy security issues.

Questions

1. *MD5 | SHA1 | XOR | ARC4*—these are the insecure code indicators for which one of the following?
    1. Weak Encryption
    2. Insecure protocol
    3. Hardcoded information
    4. Command injection

2. What kind of source code security issue can be identified with low false positive?
    1. Weak encryption
    2. Insecure protocol
    3. Weak random
    4. All of the above

3. What APIs are risky to command injection?
    1. `system`
    2. `execl`
    3. `ShellExecute`
    4. All of the above

4. What can lead to XXE injection?
    1. Failing to disable the external DTD configuration

2. No prepared statement
3. The use of eval
4. No output encoding

5. What APIs are related to XXE handling?
    1. `SAXParser`
    2. `SchemaFactory`
    3. `DocumentBuilderFactoryImpl`
    4. All of the above

6. Which of these is a correct statement about the deserialization security issue?
    1. Serialization is the process in Java of converting the state of an object into a byte stream (serialized object), which can be stored in files, memory, or a database. Deserialization is the reverse process, involving the creation of an object based on the byte stream.
    2. `readObject` is the API that may be vulnerable to a deserialization security issue.
    3. The deserialization security issue may result in an RCE attack.
    4. All of the above.

Further reading

- **SEI CERT coding standards**: https://www.securecoding.cert.org/confluence/display/seccode/SEI+CERT+Coding+Standards
- **ReBulk advanced search tool**: https://github.com/Toilal/rebulk
- **Security Development Life cycle (SDLC) banned function calls**: https://msdn.microsoft.com/en-us/library/bb288454.aspx
- **Sensitive information data type**: https://docs.microsoft.com/en-us/Exchange/policy-and-compliance/data-loss-prevention/sensitive-information-types?view=exchserver-2019#Taiwan%20National%20ID
- **Vulnerable API sample project**: https://github.com/rahulunair/vulnerable-api
- **SWAMP**: https://www.mir-swamp.org
- **Sensitive data discovery tool**: https://github.com/redglue/redsense
- **Secrets Search**: https://github.com/securing/DumpsterDiver
- **OWASP deserialization cheat sheet**: https://www.owasp.org/index.php/Deserialization_Cheat_Sheet

4
Sensitive Information and Privacy Testing

After discussing how to review the security of your code, we will now discuss how to use automated scanning to prevent the disclosure of sensitive information for every software release. There are three typical scenarios related to data privacy handling. The first is where sensitive information is included in the source code, such as an API key, a hardcoded password, a hidden hotkey, an email address, or an IP or URL. Secondly, sensitive information can also be stored in cookies, since cookies can collect the browsing behaviors of users. Finally, large projects handling massive amounts of data require effective ways of identifying and protecting any **Personal Identifiable Information** (**PII**) stored in the database.

The following is what we will be covering in this chapter:

- The objective of sensitive information testing
- Automated sensitive information scanning in the source code
- Automated sensitive information scanning for the application and database

The objective of sensitive information testing

In addition to secure code patterns, we also need to pay attention to the potential disclosure of sensitive information in our software releases. The identification of any PII helps us to investigate how the system is handling this sensitive data and see whether there is any violation of legislation, such as the **General Data Protection Regulation** (**GDPR**). Furthermore, the purpose of scanning for system-related sensitive information leakage is to review any system vulnerability exposure, such as that of a password or API key.

The following table shows details about scanning for sensitive information, PII, and the source code:

Area of white-box scanning	Objective	The primary scope of the scan
Sensitive information scanning for system information	To ensure no leaking of sensitive information, such as an API key, a password, or hardcoded administrator account credentials	Settings Installed components Scripts
Privacy scanning for handling PII	To review how PII is stored, handled, presented, and removed	Database Storage Configuration
Secure code scanning	To ensure the source code complies with secure coding rules, and to mitigate OWASP Top 10 security issues	Source code

PII discovery

Understanding where and how PII is stored is the first step for the proper protection of private data. To proceed with PII data discovery, we will discuss some simple methods of searching for any PII that may be stored on the system. Generally, PII can be stored anywhere in an application or system. PII may even be found in the recycle bin. Discovering and protecting PII requires constant effort and due diligence. The purpose of PII data discovery is to find answers to the following questions:

- What types of PII are present (such as names, emails, or other personal information)?
- Where is the PII stored (could be a database, files, or configuration)?
- How is the PII classified?
- What access permissions are there to the PII?

One common and simple approach to PII discovery is using regular expressions. The following table lists examples of regular expression patterns we may use to search the source code, configuration, and log files:

PII-related information	Examples of regular expression patterns
Credit card number	`\d{4}[ -]?\d{4}[ -]?\d{4}[ -]?\d{4}|\d{4}[ -]?\d{6}[ -]?\d{4}\d?`
Email address	`/([a-z0-9_\-.+]+)@\w+(\.\w+)*`
IP address	`\b(?:\d{1,3}\.){3}\d{1,3}\b`
Credentials	`1234	admin	password	pass	creds	login`
Phone number	`(\(?\+?[0-9]{1,2}\)?[-. ]?)?(\(?[0-9]{3}\)?|[0-9]{3})[-. ]?([0-9]{3}[-. ]?[0-9]{4}|\b[A-Z0-9]{7}\b)`
Address	`(street|st|road|rd|avenue|ave|drive|dr|loop|court|ct|circle|cir|lane|ln|boulevard|blvd|way)\.?\b`
Social security number	`\b\d{3}[ -.]?\d{2}[ -.]?\d{4}\b`
ZIP code	`\b\d{5}\b(-\d{4})?\b`
URL	`([^\s:/?#]+):\/\/([^/?#\s]*)([^?#\s]*)(\?([^#\s]*))?(#([^\s]*))?`
Dates (MM/DD/YYYY)	`^([1][12]|[0]?[1-9])[\/-]([3][01]|[12]\d|[0]?[1-9])[\/-](\d{4}|\d{2})$`

Sensitive information discovery

In addition to PII, there is also other sensitive information related to the system and applications that needs to be discovered and secured. The purpose of identifying these is to avoid such information, which may be hardcoded in the source code or within the configuration files, being exposed to debug logs:

System-related sensitive/vulnerable information	Examples of regular expression patterns
Password	`Passw(d|ord)?|secret	username	key`
Private key	`(private|api|secret|aws)[_-]?key`
Hardcoded URL	`(http | https | ftp | ftps)`
MD5 hash	`^[a-f0-9]{32}$`
SHA1 hash	`\b([a-f0-9]{40})\b`

Base64 encoding	`^(?:[A-Za-z0-9+/]{4})*`
	`(?:[A-Za-z0-9+/]{2}==|`
	`[A-Za-z0-9+/]{3}=|`
	`[A-Za-z0-9+/]{4})$`

SQL statements	`(SELECT\s[\w\*\)\`
	`(\,\s]+\sFROM\s[\w]+)|`
	`(UPDATE\s[\w]+\sSET\s[\w\,\'\=]+)|`
	`(INSERT\sINTO\s[\d\w]+[\s\w\d\)\`
	`(\,]*\sVALUES\s\([\d\w\'\,\)]+)`

Private IP	`(^127\.)|(^10\.)|(^172\.1[6-9]\.)|`
	`(^172\.2[0-9]\.)|`
	`(^172\.3[0-1]\.)|(^192\.168\.)`

Here are just some more details about what we'll be searching for and why:

- A hardcoded URL in the source code or a private IP defined in the source code can potentially become a backdoor.
- MD5, SHA1, and Base64 are weak encryption/encoding algorithms. Any passwords encoded by Base64 or hashed by MD5 and SHA1, will be at high risk.
- For SQL statements, we will be looking for whether there are any missing prepare statements and any sensitive information queries.

Privacy search tools

Using regular expression patterns is the first step in building your own secure code scanning service. It's easy to use GREP to quickly search for specified patterns. In the next sections, we will introduce three tools that can make these search jobs easier:

Tool name	Key characteristics
The Silver Searcher	This works similarly to Linux GREP for full-text searches in files, but it's much faster. It can support multiple platforms and is easy to use: `https://github.com/ggreer/the_silver_searcher`.
ReDataSense	This is useful for searching for PII in a MySQL database or in files. It can also define flexible search patterns/rules. It's a Java program but can also support multiple platforms: `https://github.com/redglue/redsense`.
DumpsterDiver	This is used to search for secrets, API keys, and encrypted passwords by using entropy. It can search logs, files, and compressed archives, and can also customize scanning rules: `https://github.com/securing/DumpsterDiver`.

Case study – weak encryption search

Let's still use the same project, the Python Vulnerable API, to search for weak encryption used in the source code. In this case, we will be looking for the uses of the vulnerable MD5 algorithm in the source code. The tool we introduce here is The Silver Searcher, which can do a fast recursive search based on a given keyword for all file contents, and indicate the results.

Step 1 – installing The Silver Searcher

The Silver Searcher providers installation details for different platforms: `https://github.com/ggreer/the_silver_searcher`.

For Windows releases, the tool can be downloaded here: `https://github.com/k-takata/the_silver_searcher-win32/releases`.

Step 2 – executing the tool (using Windows as an example)

Use `ag -h` to display all the options and usage in the console. In this case, we will use `-w` to match the keyword, `md5`. The AG tool can be executed as follows:

```
$ ag -w md5 d:\<targetPath>
```

Step 3 – reviewing the results (using Windows as an example)

The following screenshot shows the output of the tool. It shows that the `vAPI.py` file contains the `md5` keyword in three lines.

There are also other options to support various kinds of search. Just type `ag` to see the output in the console:

```
d:\myPython/vulnerable-api-master/ansible/roles/api/files/vAPI.py
9:5.  Token string is generated with an md5 of the expire datetime string
85:             token = hashlib.md5(expire_date).hexdigest()
102:            token = hashlib.md5(expire_date).hexdigest()
```

Case study – searching for a private key

Let's take another case to look at searching for the compromise of API key information. An API key being hardcoded in the source code or a password being weakly encrypted in the source code are both common security vulnerabilities. To search for a private encryption key or hardcoded password requires the calculation of entropy which is a number to represent the level of randomness. A string with a high entropy value is normally an indicator of a potential API key, hash value, or encrypted message. In the following demonstration, we will also use the vulnerable Python API project to search for vulnerable API keys in the source code. The tools we will be using are entropy.py and DumpsterDiver. To download the script, execute the following command:

```
$ git clone https://github.com/securing/DumpsterDiver
```

Step 1 – calculating the entropy

This step of entropy calculation is optional. However, an entropy value will help to improve the accuracy of the search result. For example, say we know of one other API key in the source code. Knowing the entropy value of that known API key will help to identify another unknown key with higher accuracy. In this case, we're assuming the known API key is ZeXvRCRZ3LF:

```
$ python entropy.py    ZeXvRCRZ3LF
```

The output of the entropy calculation will be done by DumpsterDiver. The entropy value of the known API key string is 3.095795255 bits. Once we have the exact entropy value of the known API key, we can search for the same entropy value of other API Keys.

Step 2 – Searching for high-entropy strings

Based on the entropy value, we can search all the projects for similar entropy values of 3.095. Again, this is optional; it just helps us to locate what we are looking for more accurately. If the entropy value is not specified, DumpsterDiver will just list all the high-entropy value strings:

```
$ python DumpsterDiver.py   --entropy 3.095  -p  <TargetProjectPath>
```

Step 3 – Reviewing the results

DumpsterDiver will list all the identified entropy strings. Then, it may need to check whether any of them indicate private API key leakage. For example, the following screenshot shows three strings with the same entropy value having been identified. We can further review whether these are exposed API keys:

```
FOUND HIGH ENTROPY!!!
The following string: com/ichernev/ed58f76fb95205eeac653d719972b90c has been found in /home/
osboxes/django-DefectDojo/components/node_modules/moment/CHANGELOG.md
()
FOUND HIGH ENTROPY!!!
The following string: com/ichernev/17bffc1005a032cb1a8ac4c1558b4994 has been found in /home/
osboxes/django-DefectDojo/components/node_modules/moment/CHANGELOG.md
()
FOUND HIGH ENTROPY!!!
The following string: com/ichernev/18e1c5bf647545c72ca30e9628a09ed3 has been found in /home/
osboxes/django-DefectDojo/components/node_modules/moment/CHANGELOG.md
()
```

Case study – website privacy inspection

Here we will look at how to identify vulnerabilities in private information when a web service goes live.

The insecure design of a website may result in the leaking or interception of private information. One of the most common ways in which information leakage can occur is by the use of insecure communication protocols, such as HTTP, Telnet, or FTP. These protocols are communicating messages without any encryption. The web administrator will need an automatic privacy scanning tool to do see whether this is an issue affecting them.

Here we introduce the use of PrivacyScore. It provides the following privacy inspections:

Privacy scan scenarios	Examples
No Track: No Browsing histories tracked by websites and third parties	• Checks whether third-party embeds are being used • Checks whether Google Analytics is being used • Checks whether the web server geo-location is based on DNS IP lookup
EncWeb: Encryption of web traffic	• Checks whether the server is running with HTTPS • Checks for automatic redirection to HTTPS
Attacks: Protection against various attacks	• Checks for HTTP security headers, such as X-Frame-Options, **Content Security Policy** (CSP), **Cross-site scripting** (XSS) protection, X-Content-Type-Options, and referrer-policy
EncMail: Encryption of mail traffic	• Checks for the DNS if the domain also includes an email server

For a quick demo of how to use PrivacyScore, you can use the online version to scan a vulnerable website. If the web service you are developing can't be reached over the internet, PrivacyScore also provides a standalone version that you can set up in house.

Step 1 – visiting PrivacyScore or setting it up locally

For the online version of PrivacyScore, please visit `https://privacyscore.org/`.

To set up PrivacyScore locally, refer to `https://github.com/PrivacyScore/PrivacyScore/`.

Input the target vulnerable website, `http://hackazon.webscantest.com/`, and click **SCAN**, as shown in the following screenshot. The scanning will be triggered and will run on the cloud:

Step 2 – reviewing the results

After the scanning is done, you will see the scanning results as follows. In our example, the website shows potential risks for the NoTrack and Attacks categories. It suggests that the web administrator take further actions to review the third-party embeds, the uses of HTTPS everywhere, and also the secure configuration of HTTP security headers:

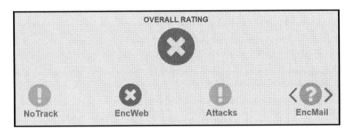

Summary

We discussed the objective of testing for sensitive information in this chapter. In terms of privacy testing, the GDPR is the primary baseline we will comply with. Privacy testing is focused on how PII is handled, and it's important to identify any risks of system-related sensitive information, such as passwords, API keys, or private IPs, being leaked. We looked at some patterns that help in searching for PII as well as sensitive system-related information.

We then looked at three case studies. The first case study was about searching for weak encryption using The Silver Searcher. The second case was about identifying potential API key leakage in the source code by using DumpsterDiver. The final case was about examining website privacy, looking specifically at the use of PrivacyScore to scan the target website.

We have practiced various kinds of white-box source code review techniques for sensitive information. In Chapter 5, *Security API and Fuzz Testing*, we will explore API security testing with fuzzing.

Questions

1. Which one of the following does not apply to white-box scanning?
   - **Web UI** testing
   - Privacy scanning PII
   - Secure code scanning

2. What is the objective of PII discovery?
   - To discern the types of PII
   - To see how the PII is classified
   - **All of above**

3. What is the regular expression for IP address?
   - `/([a-z0-9_\-.+]+)@\w+(\.\w+)*`
   - `\d{4}[ -]?\d{4}[ -]?\d{4}[ -]?\d{4}|\d{4}[ -]?\d{6}[ -]?\d{4}\d?`
   - **`\b(?:\d{1,3}\.){3}\d{1,3}\b`**

4. Why are we looking for Base64 encoding?
   - **Any password encoded with Base64 is very vulnerable and can be easily reversed**
   - To ensure there is no possibility of injection attack
   - To avoid backdoor connection behavior

Further reading

- The Silver Searcher: `https://github.com/ggreer/the_silver_searcher`
- A web privacy measurement framework: `https://github.com/citp/OpenWPM`
- PrivacyScore project: `https://github.com/PrivacyScore/PrivacyScore`
- Common Regex: `https://github.com/madisonmay/CommonRegex`
- De-identification: `https://github.com/vmenger/deduce`
- PII search: `https://technet.microsoft.com/en-us/library/2008.04.securitywatch.aspx`
- Python Vulnerable API: `https://github.com/rahulunair/vulnerable-api/`
- StaCoAn cross-platform static code analysis: `https://github.com/vincentcox/StaCoAn`

5
Security API and Fuzz Testing

n After the privacy and sensitive information security inspection, we will now explore API and fuzz testing. As the cloud software release can be on an API-level basis, there can be hundreds of APIs released at a time. The software development team will definitely need an effective way to automate the security testing for every API release. In this chapter, we will elaborate further with the help of an example by using an online pet store for how to build your automated API security testing framework with various tools. The API security testing focuses mainly on the data injection and abnormal payload. Therefore, the Fuzz testing will also be introduced as random data input and security injection for the automated API security testing.

The following topics will be discussed in this chapter:

- Automated security testing for every API release
- How to build your security API and fuzz testing framework with ZAP, JMeter, and FuzzDB

Automated security testing for every API release

Some of the web services are released with standard REST or SOAP APIs. The key difference between web and API security testing is the browser UI dependency. In API testing, we will only focus on the request and response instead of the UI layout or presentation.

It is always recommended to use the API testing approach because web UI testing can provide unreliable testing results. General API security testing may cover authentication, authorization, input validation, error handling, data protection, secure transmission, and HTTP header security.

The case we will discuss here concerns a development manager who would like to build an API security testing framework for every release. However, he may encounter the following challenges when he is trying to build the API security testing framework, especially for a development team without experienced security expertise. In the following sections, we will demonstrate some open source tools and approaches to solving these issues.

- **Data input**: API security testing requires purpose-built random security testing data (payload)
- **Process request**: This requires a proper framework to process the data input, to send the requests to web server, and process the responses
- **Process response**: To identify if any security vulnerabilities exist based on the responses. For the web API, the typical standard responses are JSON or XML instead of HTML, JavaScript, or CSS

For Fuzz data input as security payloads, refer to the following resources:

- **FuzzDB**: `https://github.com/fuzzdb-project/fuzzdb`
- **SecLists**: `https://github.com/danielmiessler/SecLists`
- **Radamsa**: `https://github.com/vah13/radamsa/releases`

Radamsa is a fuzz data payloads generator based on a specified format or data sample. It can help if you expect to generate a lot of random and unexpected data payloads:

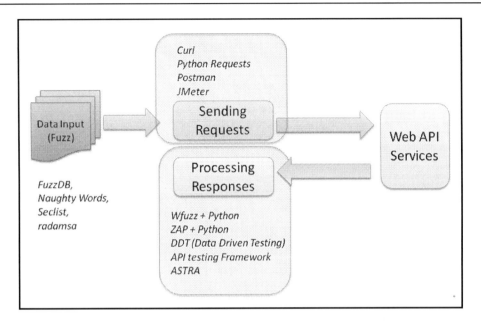

Fuzz Testing Tools

To process the HTTP requests and responses, we will use JMeter and ZAP in our demonstration cases.

Building your security API testing framework

There are several approaches and open source tools that can help to build your API security testing framework. The key challenge for security testing is the `processing responses` part. For example, to be able to identify the SQL injection vulnerability, the security testing requires not only proper designed injection payloads, but also the ability to identify the responses for SQL injection patterns. Therefore, when we build the security testing for restful or SOAP APIs, it's recommended that you apply the web security testing framework to help with the response detection.

To build the security API testing framework, we will introduce three levels of approaches as summarized in the following table:

Level	Recommended toolkits	Pros and cons
Basic	ZAP	ZAP can provide a general web security baseline scan. However, ZAP can't do specific REST or SOAP API security testing without proper guidance. For example, the HTTP POST request testing can't be done here, and that's why we introduce JMeter for the next level.
Intermediate	ZAP + JMeter	The rationale we introduce JMeter is to send specific REST or SOAP APIs and message body through ZAP. In this approach, ZAP will be running in proxy mode to monitor and detect the request/response for security issues.
Advanced	ZAP + JMeter + fuzz data	We will use JMeter with parameterized testing (data-driven testing). The fuzz data is a dictionary list of specific security issues, such as XSS, SQL injection, or common vulnerable passwords. Although ZAP itself also includes the fuzz testing that can replace the specified parameters with fuzz data, ZAP fuzz testing can only be done by GUI mode at this moment. By using ZAP and JMeter, we can execute the automation in command console mode for the integration with other CI frameworks.
Advanced	ZAP + OpenAPI	In this case, ZAP will import the API definition files, and do the initial security assessment based on the API lists.

Case study 1 – basic – web service testing with ZAP CLI

In this case, we will demonstrate how to execute ZAP using the **command line interface (CLI)**, which provides a simple way to trigger the security testing and can be easily integrated with other frameworks. The key steps of the web security scanning include spider scan, active scan, and review the scan results.

Step 1 – OWASP ZAP download and launch with port 8090

The OWASP ZAP installer can be downloaded at `https://github.com/zaproxy/zaproxy/wiki/Downloads` depending on the platform. Once the installation is done, launch ZAP in GUI mode. Although ZAP can also be executed in daemon mode, the GUI mode will help us to review the security assessment results. By default, the ZAP CLI is using the default port `8090` with ZAP. The proxy settings for ZAP can be configured using the menu under the **Tools** | **Options** | **Local Proxies** | **Port** | `8090`, as shown in the following screenshot:

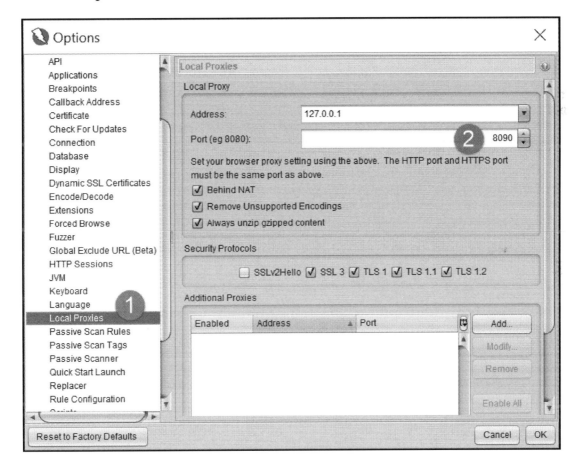

OWASP ZAP proxy configuration

Step 2 – install the ZAP-CLI

ZAP provides several non-GUI interfaces for integration, such as Java API, REST API, and CLI. You may choose one of them for the integration. We will use ZAP-CLI here because it's easy to set up, and is also suitable for engineers who have a little programming background. Please ensure Python and PIP are installed on the system. The ZAP-CLI can be installed by one command line, as follows:

```
$ pip install --upgrade zapcli
```

To access ZAP using ZAP-CLI or ZAP, restful API will require an API Key. The API key of ZAP can be found or disabled under **Tools** | **Options** | **API**. To simplify the ZAP-CLI operations, we will disable the API key.

Step 3 – execute the testing under ZAP-CLI

Once ZAP and the ZAP-CLI setup are done, we may trigger a few security assessments. Please be reminded that a spider scan is a must before running an active scan. Here are the differences between spider, quick, and active scans:

- **Spider Scan**: It will explore and search all possible resources and URLs of the website. No security attacks will be performed.
- **Active Scan**: It will do security checks based on URLs or web resources available in the ZAP site tree. Therefore, a spider scan to explore web resources is a must before an active scan.
- **Quick Scan**: It's an all-in-one command that can do a spider scan, active scan and generate a testing report.

To trigger the security scanning with the ZAP-CLI, execute the commands in the following order:

```
$ zap-cli   spider        http://demo.testfire.net
$ zap-cli   quick-scan    http://demo.testfire.net
$ zap-cli   active-scan   http://demo.testfire.net
```

If it works well, you should be able to see the list of scanned URLs and alters in the ZAP GUI.

For other command options, the `--help` can be used, as follows:

```
$ zap-cli --help
```

For example, the following command will help you to know how to use of `active-scan`:

```
$ zap-cli   active-scan   --help
```

Refer to the following link for the detailed usage of the ZAP-CLI:

```
https://github.com/Grunny/zap-cli
```

Step 4 – review the results

You can the security assessment results in the ZAP GUI console or generate a report. Alternatively, you can also output the security findings by using the ZAP-CLI. The following command will output the alerts at the medium level:

```
$ zap-cli alerts -l Medium
```

For the usage of `alerts` options, try the following command:

```
$ zap-cli   alerts   --help
```

Case study 2 – intermediate – API testing with ZAP and JMeter

In this case, we will do the login testing scenario to demonstrate the uses of JMeter with ZAP. If the team has done the automation testing by JMeter, the ZAP can work well with JMeter. In this scenario, JMeter will be used to send HTTP POST with username and password parameters to the target vulnerable website, and ZAP will be monitoring security issue through the HTTP requests and responses in proxy mode. Based on the previously installed ZAP environment, we will set up JMeter for the testing.

The following diagram shows the frameworks relationship between JMeter and ZAP:

JMeter and ZAP security testing

To proceed with the testing, follow these steps.

Step 1 – download JMeter

JMeter can be downloaded from `Https://jmeter.apache.org/download_jmeter.cgi`. Java 8 runtime is required to execute JMeter. It's a compressed package. Once it's downloaded, unzip the package. To launch JMeter, run the `jmeter.bat` (Windows) or `jmeter.sh` (Linux), which can be found under `\bin` folder.

Step 2 – define HTTP request for the login

In this step, we will define the HTTP POST request for login to the vulnerable website. Here is key information of the HTTP POST request for the login. It's assumed that the username is `user1` and the password is `pass1` in this example. The information can be acquired by using browser network inspector (*F12*), as follows:

```
Request URL:  http://demo.testfire.net/bank/login.aspx
Request Method: POST
Request Data: uid=user1&passw=pass1&btnSubmit=Login
```

To configure JMeter to send the HTTP POST login request, we need to create a `Threat Group` and the `HTTP Request` for the test plan. Under the HTTP request, define the values as shown in the following screenshot:

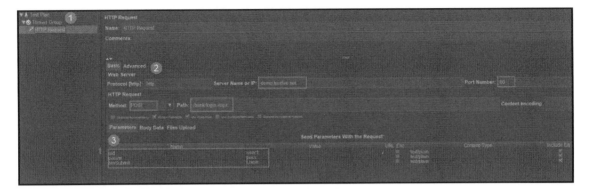

HTTP request configuration in JMeter

In addition, we would like to send the HTTP request through the ZAP proxy. Define the JMeter proxy in the **Advanced** tab. In our environment, we are running ZAP listening port `8090`:

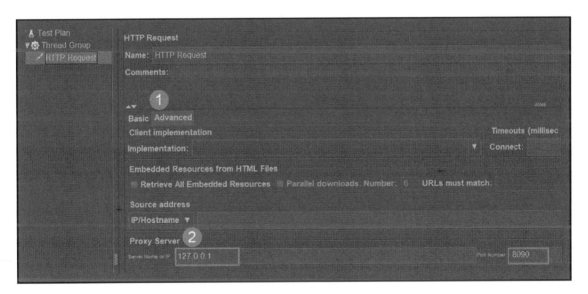

HTTP request proxy configuration in JMeter

Step 4 – execute the JMeter script

There are two ways to run the JMeter script. One involves using the menu, and the other involves using the command console. Once the information is properly defined, send the request by **Run** | **Start** or *Ctrl + R*. The HTTP POST request will be sent through the ZAP proxy and ZAP will intercept the request and response for security assessments. Once we have done the automation scripts with JMeter, it's suggested to execute the JMeter in non-GUI mode for further automation integration. In our case, the following command will apply to our JMeter script. Use JMeter –help to see further information of each command options:

```
Jmeter  -n  -t  MyRequest.jmx  -l  testResult.jtl  -H 127.0.0.1  -P 8090
```

Step 3 – review the results in ZAP

We can review the initial security assessments done by the OWASP ZAP under **Alerts** tab. Alternatively, execute one of the following command in the console. It will list the security assessments results in JSON or HTML format, as follows:

```
$ CURL   "http://localhost:8090/JSON/core/view/alerts"
```

The following command will generate the ZAP alerts report in HTML format:

```
$ CURL   "http://localhost:8090/HTML/core/view/alerts"
```

Case study 3 – advanced – parameterized security payload with fuzz

In this testing scenario, we are going to replace the username and password with security payloads, such as XXE, XSS, or SQL injection attacks. To test if the login is vulnerable to SQL injection, JMeter will be reading the external fuzz SQL injection data to replace the username and password parameters to send the login request.

To generate a list of security payloads, here are some of the recommended resources:

Fuzz database	Description
FuzzDB	FuzzDB compressive application security testing dictionary for attack patterns (injection, XSS, directory traversals), discovery (admin directories or sensitive files), response analysis (regular expression patterns), web backdoor samples, and user/pwd list. `https://github.com/fuzzdb-project/fuzzdb`
Naughty Strings	The Naughty Strings provides a very long list of strings. There are two formats provided, `blns.txt` and `blns.json`. `https://github.com/minimaxir/big-list-of-naughty-strings`
SecList	This is similar to FuzzDB, which provides various kinds of fuzz data such as command injections, JSON, LDAP, user agents, XSS, char, numeric, Unicode data, and so on `https://github.com/danielmiessler/SecLists`
Radamsa	Unlike previous FuzzDB that provides a list of word dictionary, it's a tool that can dynamically generate format-specific based on a given sample `https://github.com/vah13/radamsa`

Follow the following instructions to apply the SQL injection data with JMeter.

Step 1 – download the SQL injection data

To replace the parameter password with the SQL injection payloads, we can use the FuzzDB or SecList resources in the previous list. For example, SecLists provides a list of SQL injection payloads we can use. The following table lists common SQL injection security payloads that can be obtained from the following URL:

`https://github.com/danielmiessler/SecLists/blob/master/Fuzzing/Generic-SQLi.txt`.

In this case, we will create the `sqli.csv` with the SQL injection security payloads, as follows:

SQL injection payloads samples
| ```
UNION ALL SELECT
 ) or sleep(__TIME__)='
)) or benchmark(10000000,MD5(1))#
hi' or 'a'='a
0
21 %
limit
or 1=1
or 2 > 1
``` |

Step 2 – define the CSV dataset in JMeter

To add a CSV dataset, right-click the **Test Plan** | **Add** | **Config Element** | **CSV Data Set Config**. In the **CSV Data Set Config**, we can define the data input source from the `sqli.csv` files and variable names.

The following screenshot shows the **CSV Data Set Config** in JMeter that is used to read the values from the `sqli.csv`:

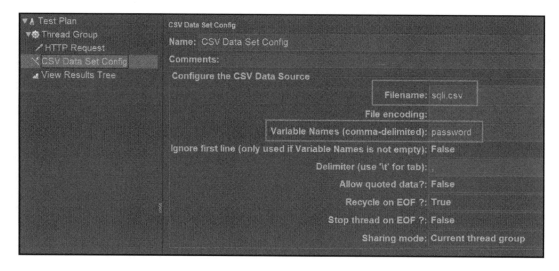

CSV Data Set Config in JMeter
```

Step 3 – apply the variable name

In our original JMeter script, we will replace the value of password to the defined variable name ${password} as mentioned in the previous step:

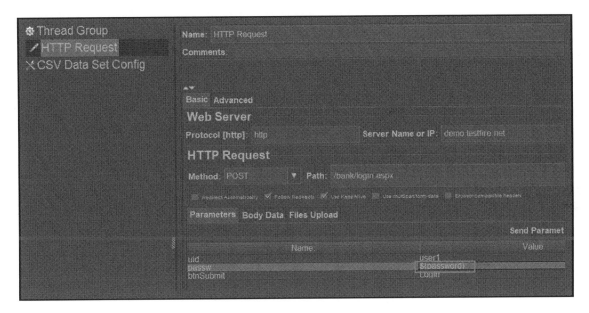

Defined variables in HTTP request in JMeter

Step 4 – specify the loop

Finally, we define the number of loops we would like to send to the HTTP requests with the parameterized data. In our example, we define loop count as `10`:

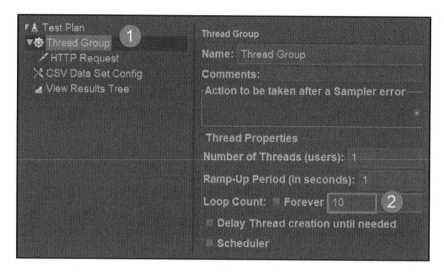

Thread group in JMeter

Step 5 – execute JMeter and review the security assessment results

Follow the following command to execute the JMeter script with ZAP proxy `1270.0.1:8090`:

```
$ Jmeter  -n  -t  MyRequest.jmx  -l  testResult.jtl  -H 127.0.0.1  -P 8090
```

Under the OWAZP GUI console, the security assessment will be listed in the **Alerts** tab. In this case, the SQL injection vulnerability was identified. If we review the **Alerts** in the ZAP, we can see the **Application Error Disclosure**, which is also an indicator of error-based SQL injection vulnerability. To view the alerts, we can also use the following commands to output to the console or specified files:

```
CURL "http://localhost:8090/JSON/core/view/alerts" > LoginTesting.JSON

CURL "http://localhost:8090/HTML/core/view/alerts" > LoginTesting.HTML
```

The following diagram shows the **Alerts** after sending the SQL injection payloads to the login API, especially the **Application Error Disclosure** parts:

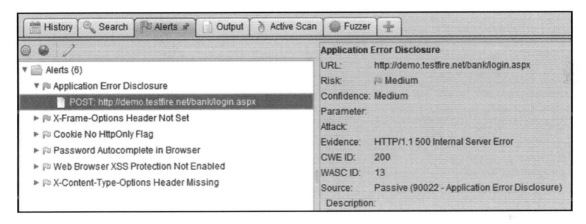

Error disclosure in ZAP

In this case, we target the login API for the testing of SQL injection vulnerability. We apply JMeter to read external FuzzDB resources for the SQL injection data input and define the CSV data in JMeter for the parameterized testing of the password variable. Once the various SQL injection data payloads were sent by JMeter through the ZAP proxy, we review the security assessments in ZAP. Other security payloads, such as XSS, XXE, or command injection, can also apply to the same login API for further testing. On the other hand, we can use similar approaches to test other APIs.

Case study 4 – security testing with ZAP Open/SOAP API

Some web services may provide a list of REST or SOAP API interfaces. These API interfaces are built for other application to do further integration or customization. The standard response of the REST or SOAP APIs can be JSON or XML. ZAP can be installed with the OpenAPI and SOAP API add-ons for the web API security testing. Take the PetStore API as an example: `https://petstore.swagger.io/`. In this case, ZAP can import the API definition files and assess security issue for every API. This is the most effective way to ensure that all the APIs are included in the ZAP scanning. Simply doing the spider scanning in ZAP won't enable you to list all the API interfaces.

Step 1 – install the OpenAPI and SOAP API add-ons

To enable the API definition import features, ZAP will need to additionally install two add-ons. Execute the following command in the console:

```
Zap -addoninstall soap -addoninstall openapi
```

If the installation is successful, the following command will be able to output the HTML message in the console:

```
CURL "http://localhost:8090/UI/openapi/"
```

Step 2 – import the API definition

ZAP can import the API definition by a local file or URL Taking the PetStore API as an example, we provide the URL for `swagger.json` in the `CURL importUrl` command options. Please be aware that the following command should be in one line without any line break, although it may look like two lines due to the layout formatting:

```
CURL
"http://localhost:8090/JSON/openapi/action/importUrl/?zapapiformat=JSON&for
mMethod=GET&url=https://petstore.swagger.io/v2/swagger.json&hostOverride="
```

It may take a while to import the APIs. Once it's done, you will see the API list in the ZAP console as shown in the following diagram:

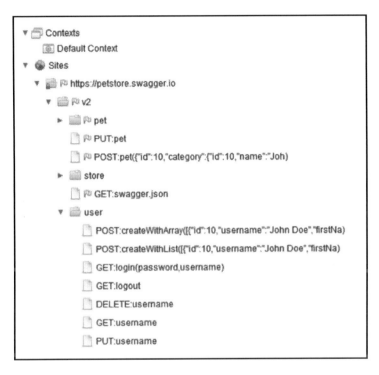

API security in ZAP

Alternatively, you can also import the API by browser using the following URL:

```
http://localhost:8090/UI/openapi/action/importUrl/
```

Step 3 – execute the active security scanning

We can use `ascan` to do the active scanning for the PetStore website. Refer to the following command:

```
CURL
"http://localhost:8090/JSON/ascan/action/scan/?zapapiformat=JSON&formMethod=
GET&url=https://petstore.swagger.io/&recurse=&inScopeOnly=&scanPolicyName=&
method=&postData=&contextId="
```

Step 4 – present the security assessments

Once the active scanning is done, view the `alerts` for the assessments results. It can be in either JSON or HTML formats, as follows:

```
$  CURL "http://localhost:8090/JSON/core/view/alerts"
$  CURL   "http://localhost:8090/HTML/core/view/alerts"
```

For the advanced user who would like to filter the output with specific URL, refer to the following command:

```
$ CURL
"http://localhost:8090/JSON/core/view/alerts/?zapapiformat=JSON&formMethod=
GET&baseurl=https://petstore.swagger.io&start=&count=&riskId="
```

The following command will generate HTML format results:

```
$ CURL
"http://localhost:8090/HTML/core/view/alerts/?zapapiformat=HTML&formMethod=
GET&baseurl=https://petstore.swagger.io&start=&count=&riskId="
```

Summary

In this chapter, we discussed the security testing for API release. The API security testing involved the data input, the requests, and the analysis of the responses. For the data input parts, we suggested using FuzzDB and SecList. To send the API requests, we applied the OWASP ZAP and JMeter in our case studies. For the security analysis of API responses, we used OWASP ZAP.

Four hands-on case studies were demonstrated. They applied different techniques for the API security testing scenarios. In addition, we also demonstrated how the testing tool JMeter can be integrated with the security scanning tool ZAP to achieve the API security testing:

- Basic—web service testing with ZAP CLI
- Intermediate—API testing with ZAP and JMeter
- Advanced—parameterized security payload with fuzz
- Security testing with ZAP OpenAPI/SOAP API

After having discussed API-level security testing, we will move on to the integrated security testing of web applications in the next chapter.

Questions

1. Which one of the followings is not used for security data payloads source?
    1. FuzzDB
    2. SecLists
    3. CURL
    4. Naughty Strings

2. Which one can be used to send HTTP requests?
    1. JMeter
    2. Python Requests
    3. CURL
    4. All of above

3. Which one of the ZAP-CLI commands can be used to trigger the security assessments?
    1. ZAP-CLI spider
    2. ZAP-CLI quick-scan
    3. ZAP-CLI active-scan
    4. All of above

4. In JMeter, what element is used to read the CSV values?
    1. CSV Data Set Config
    2. HTTP Request
    3. View Results Tree
    4. Thread Group

5. What will the ZAP API do?
    1. View the testing results?
    2. Trigger a testing
    3. Spider a website

Further reading

- **ASTRA API Security Testing**: https://www.astra-security.info
- **API Security Checklist**: https://github.com/shieldfy/API-Security-Checklist
- **Python API Security testing by OpenStack Security**: https://github.com/openstack/syntribos
- **Testing your API for Security in Python**: https://github.com/BBVA/apitest
- **Online Vulnerable Web**: http://website zero.webappsecurity.com
- **FuzzDB**: https://github.com/fuzzdb-project/fuzzdb
- **SecList**: https://github.com/danielmiessler/SecLists
- **Web Security Fuzz Testing 0d1n**: https://github.com/CoolerVoid/0d1n

6
Web Application Security Testing

In this chapter, we will use an online shopping site, Hackazon, to demonstrate how to achieve automated web security testing. The key challenge in automating web application testing is walking through the UI business flow while doing a security inspection; for example, using automated testing to look at user sign-in/sign-out, or to add items to shopping carts while scanning for potential **cross-site scripting** (**XSS**) injection vulnerabilities for every data input. Tackling this challenge requires not only security scanning but also web UI automation. We will be using security tools, such as ZAP, and also web UI automation frameworks, such as Selenium and Robot Framework. Using both of these tools can effectively improve your security testing coverage. We will share some tips and tools to make web automation easier.

In this chapter, we will cover the following topics:

- Online shopping site for automated security inspection
- Case 1—web security testing using the ZAP REST API
- Case 2—full automation with CURL and the ZAP daemon
- Case 3—automated security testing for the user registration flow using Selenium

Case study – online shopping site for automated security inspection

We will be using the vulnerable website Hackazon to demonstrate automation security testing techniques: `http://hackazon.webscantest.com/`. We will be using three cases to explore the testing scenario and automation techniques, which are listed in the following table:

Case scenario	Security testing objective	Security automation techniques
Case 1—web security testing using the ZAP REST API	General web security assessments	• ZAP active scanning mode • Use of the ZAP REST API
Case 2—full automation with CURL and the ZAP daemon	• Running ZAP in daemon mode • Automating the ZAP REST API and CURL	—
Case 3—automated security testing for the user registration flow	Security assessments for the user registration flow	• ZAP security assessments with proxy mode • Selenium web UI automation • ZAP with CURL REST API operations

Case 1 – web security testing using the ZAP REST API

In this case, ZAP will be running in proxy mode with port `8090`. Once ZAP is running, the ZAP web console can be reached at `http://localhost:8090/UI`. The demo website is the target website to be inspected by ZAP. We will use CURL to trigger the ZAP RESTful API to operate ZAP to do spider scans, active scans, review alerts, and shut down ZAP:

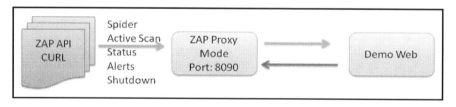

ZAP API testing in proxy mode

Step 1 – spider scanning the website

The purpose of the spider scan is to discover all resources and URLs for the target website. The spider visits these URLs and will try to identify all the hyperlinks in the responses. The scanning process continues recursively whenever new URLs are identified. All identified URLs can be used for further security inspection and active scans in the next step.

Sending the REST API request to ZAP will require the API key. To simplify the implementation, we will disable the API key in our demonstration. The API key can be disabled under the ZAP console menu, via **Tools** | **Options** | **API** | **Disable the API Key** checkbox.

Here is the command to execute the spider scan by CURL:

```
$ curl
"http://localhost:8090/JSON/spider/action/scan/?zapapiformat=JSON&formMetho
d=GET&url=http://hackazon.webscantest.com&maxChildren=&recurse=&contextName
=&subtreeOnly="
```

To get further information for the HTTP GET request for the spider scan, we can use the browser to visit the ZAP URL: `http://localhost:8090/UI/`. This provides an explanatory API document and operations. For example, we can trigger the spider scan by clicking on **spider** and **scan** (`url maxChildren recurse contextName subtreeOnly`). This will navigate us to `http://localhost:8090/UI/spider/view/scans/` (as shown in the following diagram), where we can define some parameters and trigger the scan. After the spider scan is triggered, the URL we get is the final URL (the HTTP GET request) we need for the CURL automation.

The following diagram shows the spider scan UI operations in ZAP:

ZAP API UI

Component: spider

Action: scan

Runs the spider against the given URL (or context).
spider from seeding recursively, the parameter 'cont
the specified 'url').

Output format	JSON ▾
Form method	GET ▾
url	http://hackazon.webscantes
maxChildren	
recurse	
contextName	
subtreeOnly	

scan

ZAP spider API

For Windows users, CURL can be downloaded here: `https://curl.haxx.se/windows/`.

The spider scan may take a long time since it will extensively and recursively search for any potential web URLs and resources. Besides, the time it takes also depends on the number of web pages, parameters, and the number of threads. When it takes too long to complete, you may also configure the spider scan options under **Tools** | **Options** | **Spider**, where you may configure **Maximum depth to crawl** or **Number of threads used**.

Step 2 – active scanning the website

Once we have done the spider scan, the active scan will find the security vulnerabilities by sending malicious requests, such as XSS or SQL injection, based on the scanning policies.

Here is the command to trigger the active scan with CURL:

```
$ curl
"http://localhost:8090/JSON/ascan/action/scan/?zapapiformat=JSON&formMethod
=GET&url=http://hackazon.webscantest.com&recurse=&inScopeOnly=&scanPolicyNa
me=&method=&postData=&contextId="
```

The URL of the active scan is `http://localhost:8090/UI/ascan/action/scan/`.

The key difference between the spider scan and the active scan is that the spider scan involves passive scanning, which entails monitoring security issues such as missing security headers, **cross-site request forgery (CSRF)** tokens and so on. On the other hand, the active scan will send malicious requests such as XSS or SQL injection to attack the target website. The spider scan will extensively search for web resources, and the active scan can do specific security testing based on the scan policy. During execution, using the spider scan to extensively explore the URLs and resources is the first step before triggering the active scan, since it will help the active scan with known URLs to do the security scanning:

	Spider scan	Active scan
Handling of requests and responses	It's a passive scan, which means it monitors requests and responses for the security issues.	As it's an active scan, it will send malicious requests, such as XSS or SQL injection.
Purpose	Explores the whole site and monitors security issues. It's a preliminary step for any further security scanning.	Sends malicious requests and evaluates specific security issues based on the identified URLs.

Step 3 – reviewing the status of the active scan

To review the status of the active scan, try one of the following commands. It will output the percentage of completeness as a status value. Depending on the output format you need, you may change JSON to HTML:

```
$ curl  "http://localhost:8090/JSON/ascan/view/status/"
```

The following command will generate the active scan status in JSON format:

```
$ curl
"http://localhost:8090/JSON/ascan/view/status/?zapapiformat=JSON&formMethod
=GET&scanId="
```

Step 4 – reviewing the security assessments

To review the security assessments made by OWASP ZAP, we may use one of the REST APIs, as follows:

```
$ CURL  http://localhost:8090/HTML/core/view/alerts/
```

Alternatively, the HTML report can be generated by exporting to `ZAP_Report.HTML` via the REST API, as follows:

```
$ curl
"http://127.0.0.1:8090/OTHER/core/other/htmlreport/?formMethod=GET" >
ZAP_Report.HTML
```

Case 2 – full automation with CURL and the ZAP daemon

In this case study, we will further extend the case to execute ZAP in daemon (headless) mode. We will automate the web security tests with OWASP ZAP in the following order for a complete testing cycle:

1. Launch ZAP in daemon mode
2. Spider scan the whole website
3. Active scan all the scanned URLs
4. Check status and wait for the active scan to finish
5. Shut down the ZAP daemon

Step 1 – executing ZAP in daemon (headless) mode

To launch ZAP in daemon mode, execute the following commands in the console.

For Windows, execute the following:

```
$ ZAP.bat -daemon
```

For Linux, execute the following:

```
$ ZAP.sh  -daemon
```

For ZAP command-line options and usage, refer to https://github.com/zaproxy/zap-core-help/wiki/HelpCmdline.

Step 2 – checking the status of the ZAP daemon

In our testing environment, our ZAP proxy is configured using port 8090. The proxy port can be configured from the ZAP GUI menu under **Tools** | **Options** | **Local Proxies.** Use the following commands to check if it's running normally:

```
$ Curl   http://localhost:8090/
```

Step 3 – fully automating the ZAP API

The whole scanning process can be fully automated in one script file. Here, we use the Windows BAT script as an example. The fully automated ZAP security testing script for the Hackazon website is named AutoZAP.BAT:

```
echo start the ZAP in daemon mode

ZAP.exe -daemon



echo the status of ZAP

CURL http://localhsot:8090



echo spider scan for the web site

CURL
"http://localhost:8090/JSON/spider/action/scan/?zapapiformat=JSON&formMethod=GET&url=http://hackazon.webscantest.com"



echo Active Scan for the website

CURL
```

```
"http://localhost:8090/JSON/ascan/action/scan/?zapapiformat=JSON&formMethod
=GET&url=http://hackazon.webscantest.com&recurse=&inScopeOnly=&scanPolicyNa
me=&method=&postData=&contextId="


echo Wait for 20 sec to complete the ActiveScan before generating the
testing report

echo The timeout is for Windows command. For running in Linux, please
change it to sleep.

timeout 20


echo List the security assessments results (alerts), and output the report
to ZAP_Report.HTML

CURL "http://localhost:8090/JSON/ascan/view/status/"

CURL "http://localhost:8090/HTML/core/view/alerts/"

CURL "http://127.0.0.1:8090/OTHER/core/other/htmlreport/?formMethod=GET" >
ZAP_Report.HTML


echo shutdown the ZAP

CURL
"http://localhost:8090/JSON/core/action/shutdown/?zapapiformat=JSON&formMet
hod=GET"
```

Case 3 – automated security testing for the user registration flow with Selenium

In the previous demo, we used ZAP to do a spider scan and an active scan. The purpose of the spider scan is to explore all potential URLs and web resources. However, there are some web resources that will require manual guidance, such as authenticated resources, user registration, or the shopping business flows.

Therefore, we will need a web UI automation framework, such as Selenium, to guide ZAP through some of the web pages. A testing team who may previously finish the functional automation testing, it's suggested to apply the web security scanner, OWASP ZAP, in proxy mode to reuse the existing automation testing.

In this case study, we use the user registration flow as an example to demonstrate how to apply a Selenium automation framework and ZAP for web security automation testing.

We inspect security issues for the new user registration flow for the vulnerable shopping site at `http://hackazon.webscantest.com/`. The sign-up flow, **Sign Up | New User**, is as follows. The Selenium automation framework will do the following steps:

1. Visit the home page
2. Click **Sign Up | New User**
3. Input the **First Name**, **Last Name**, **Username**, **Email Address**, **Password**, and **Confirm Password** values, and then click **Register**

During the automated user registration execution by Selenium, we will launch ZAP as a proxy to monitor the security issues:

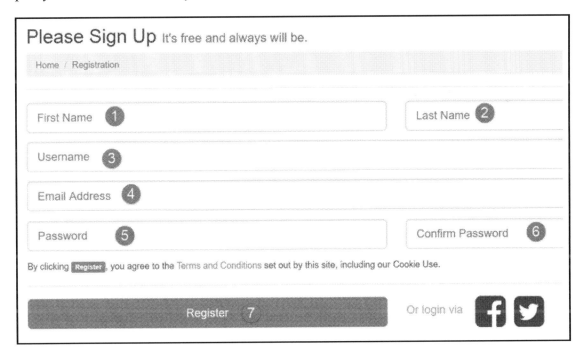

Sign Up in NodeGoat

To complete the automated security testing scenario, we will use SeleniumBase to launch the browser and simulate user behavior to guide ZAP through the registration flow, as shown in the following diagram:

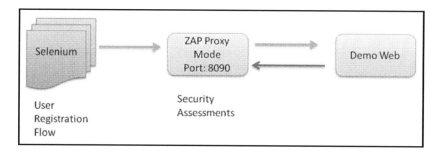

Selenium and ZAP security testing

Step 1 – installation of SeleniumBase

Prepare the environment, to have the Python and pip setup tools ready. Refer to `Http://seleniumbase.com` for the installation of SeleniumBase, which is a wrapper of Selenium to make the implementation much easier:

```
$ git clone https://github.com/seleniumbase/SeleniumBase.git
$ pip install -U -r requirements.txt
$ python setup.py install
```

In addition, Selenium will require the related browser driver to be installed, as follows:

```
$ seleniumbase install chromedriver
```

Step 2 – launching ZAP with proxy 8090

Execute the following command to launch the ZAP on port 8090:

```
$ ZAP   -port  8090
```

Step 3 – executing the user registration flow automation

The following command will help us to execute the SeleniumBase script and launch the Chrome browser with the local proxy to the running ZAP:

```
$ pytest  userregistration_SB.py   --browser=chrome   --
proxy=127.0.0.1:8090
```

Here is the script for `userregistration_SB.py`. Please be reminded that the script can only be executed by SeleniumBase, instead of Selenium.

For readers who may not be familiar with Selenium scripts, it's suggested to use the Katalon/Selenium IDE, which is a tool that allows you to record website operations and generate the script automatically. It can be installed as a Chrome or Firefox extension. In our case, we use the Katalon/Selenium IDE for the user registration flow and export in the Python 2 (WebDriver + unittest) format. Then, we use the `seleniumbase covert UserRegistration.py` command to get the following script:

```
# -*- coding: utf-8 -*-

from seleniumbase import BaseCase
class UserRegistration(BaseCase):

    def test_user_registration(self):
        self.open('http://hackazon.webscantest.com/')
        self.click("link=Sign In / Sign Up")
        self.click('#username')
        self.click("link=New user?")
        self.click('#first_name')
        self.update_text('#first_name', 'FirstName')
        self.update_text('#last_name', 'LastName')
        self.update_text('#username', 'UserName1')
        self.update_text('#email', 'abc@a.com')
        self.update_text('#password', 'pass1234')
        self.update_text('#password_confirmation', 'pass1234')
        self.click("//input[@value='Register']")
```

Step 4 – active scanning the identified URLs

After the user registration UI flow walkthrough, ZAP will be able to identify more URLs.

The active scan will be able to explore more security based on the newly identified URLs, as follows:

```
$ CURL
"http://localhost:8090/JSON/ascan/action/scan/?zapapiformat=JSON&formMethod
=GET&url=http://hackazon.webscantest.com&recurse=&inScopeOnly=&scanPolicyNa
me=&method=&postData=&contextId="
```

Step 5 – reviewing the security assessments

Once the automation execution is done, we may execute the following command to review the security assessments made by ZAP. The following RESTful API will generate the report in JSON format:

```
$ CURL "http://localhost:8090/JSON/core/view/alerts"
```

The following RESTful API will generate the report in HTML format:

```
$ CURL "http://localhost:8090/HTML/core/view/alerts"
```

If all these steps work, we may integrate all the commands into one script for further automation execution. Here is the summary of all the automation commands in one BAT script file, "Auto_ZAP_UserRegistration.BAT". Be reminded that we add a Windows timeout command to wait for the finish of the UI automation; UserRegisterResult.html will be the final security testing results.

Execute the BAT script, "Auto_ZAP_UserRegistration.BAT" on Windows:

```
$ ZAP -port 8090
```

```
$ pytest UserRegistration.py --browser=chrome --proxy=127.0.0.1:8090
```

```
$ timeout /T 30
```

```
$ CURL
"http://localhost:8090/JSON/ascan/action/scan/?zapapiformat=JSON&formMethod
=GET&url=http://hackazon.webscantest.com&recurse=&inScopeOnly=&scanPolicyNa
me=&method=&postData=&contextId="
```

```
$ timeout /T 30
```

```
$ Curl "http://localhost:8090/HTML/core/view/alerts" >
UserRegisterResult.html
```

Summary

In this chapter, we used an online shopping platform to perform web security testing using ZAP. Two main approaches were introduced. The first was using ZAP for web security scanning, which was automated by a REST API or CLI. The other approach was the integration of ZAP and Selenium to review security issues during the user registration flow. Let's review the key learning objectives of each case.

The purpose of case 1 was to demonstrate how to automate the ZAP spider scan by using a REST API and CURL.

The objective of case 2 was to run ZAP in daemon mode and to execute a full security scan cycle in one script. The automation steps of ZAP scanning include the following:

1. Launch ZAP in daemon mode
2. Spider scan the whole website
3. Active scan all the scanned URLs
4. Check status and wait for the active scan to finish
5. Shut down the ZAP daemon

Case 3 looked at automated security testing for the user registration flow, showing how ZAP and Selenium can be integrated. We used Selenium to guide ZAP for the registration UI flow.

These three cases demonstrated different automation approaches to web security scanning. In the next chapter, we will discuss different automation approaches to Android security testing.

Questions

1. What's the typical order of a ZAP scan?
   1. Spider scan → Active scan → Alerts → Shutdown
   2. Active Scan → Spider Scan → Alerts → Shutdown
   3. Active scan → Alerts → Shutdown

2. In ZAP, what's the key difference between a spider scan and an active scan?
   1. A spider scan involves monitoring security issues in passive mode
   2. An active scan will send malicious requests
   3. An active scan does specific security testing based on the scan policy
   4. All of the above

3. Which automation framework cannot be used to automate the user registration flow?
    1. Selenium
    2. SeleniumBase
    3. All of the above

4. What can be required to execute the user registration flow automation?
    1. Selenium
    2. Selenium ChromeDriver
    3. All of the above

Further reading

- **ZAPping the Top 10**: https://www.owasp.org/index.php/ZAPpingTheTop10
- **SeleniumBase**: https://github.com/seleniumbase/SeleniumBase
- **Katalon Automation Recorder**: https://www.katalon.com/resources-center/blog/katalon-automation-recorder/
- **ZAP Blog**: http://zaproxy.blogspot.com/
- **ZAP Proxy**: https://github.com/zaproxy

Android Security Testing 7

It's common practice to perform security checks before every Android application release. However, it can be a challenge for frequent and an increasing number of releases. The automated security testing process for an Android mobile application requires the submission of APK (Android Application Package) binaries, reversing the APK for secure source code inspection, manifesting a configuration check, and generating a testing result. We will also introduce mobile security-related practices, such as OWASP (Open Web Application Security Project) mobile security testing, and Android secure coding practices.

The following topics will be covered in this chapter:

- Android security review best practices
- Secure source code review patterns for Android
- Privacy and sensitive information review
- General process of APK security analysis
- Static secure code scanning with QARK
- Automated security scanning with MobSF

Android security review best practices

Android application development is primarily based on Java. The MITRE Java secure coding rules still apply to the Android security review. In addition, the Android application includes some unique building components that may introduce new security issues, such as Android manifest configurations, intents, activity, broadcast, content provider, and services:

- Android application secure design / secure coding guidebook by JSSEC
- Android developers documentation—app security best practices
- OWASP mobile security testing guide

For common security issues of APK, the *App Security Improvement* program of the Google Android developers provides the most recent security issues and the remediation advice, such as path traversal, insecure hostname verification, and fragment injection. It's also a good reference when the APK is submitted to Google Play.

In the coming sections, we will mainly demonstrate four kinds of security and privacy scanning of a mobile application, which are listed in the following table:

Scanning approach	Automated tools	Description
Secure code scanning	Fireline	Static Java source code scanning. It's a light-weight secure code scanning tools, but it may require the Java source and the reverse of APK.
Privacy and sensitive information scan	Androwarn	It's focused on privacy and sensitive information scanning of any given APK. Static analysis of the application's Dalvik bytecode, represented as Smali for PII and sensitive information leakage or exfiltration such as telephony identifiers, geolocation information leakage, audio/video flow interception, and so on.
Light-weight all in one APK security scanning	**QARK (Quick android review kit)**	It's a Python program that can do automatic security scanning of any given APK.
All in one security scanning	**Mobile Security Framework (MobSF)**	The MobSF is similar to QARK (Quick Android Review Kit). In addition, MobSF supports Android, Windows, and iOS applications. It not only does the static security analysis, but also the dynamic runtime behavior analysis.

Secure source code review patterns for Android

The Java secure code review techniques and tools in the previous chapters still apply to the Android application. The secure Java coding is fundamental to the Android security review. On top of that, there are specific secure code review techniques for the Android application.

The following table summarizes the keywords and patterns for potential security issues we need to focus on:

Security inspection focuses	Related high-risk APIs and keywords
SQL injection	`rawQuery` | `execSQL` | `database` | `.sqlite` | `SQLiteDatabase`
Insecure SSL handling	`ALLOW_ALL_HOST_VERIFIER` | `NullHostnameVerifier` `SSLCertificateSocketFactory` | `SSLSocketFactory` `setDefaultHostnameVerifier` `WebViewClient.onReceivedSsLError`
Command injection	`getRuntime` | `ClassLoader`
WebView for XSS	`Android.webkit` | `setJavaScriptEnabled` | `addJavascriptInterface` | `setWebContentsDebuggingEnabled(true)` `loadData` | `postURL`
Insecure files I/O access	`MODE_WORLD_READABLE` | `MODE_WORLD_WRITTABLE` `OpenFileOutput` | `openORCreateDatabase` `file://` | `getSharedPreferences` | `getExternal`
Insecure communication	`.netURL` | `openSteam` | `netJarURL` | `HttpURL` |`HttpRqeuest` | `HttpsURL`

The 'OWASP Mobile App security Testing' guide provides a good reference for both static and dynamic security anlaysis techniques and tools. It includes both Android and iOS security testing guide.

Privacy and sensitive information review

The mobile app is installed on the personal phone, therefore, it's more sensitive if the application will can personal information on the phone or abuse the phone services. Whenever the privacy information is handled, we will have to review the purpose and the needs.

The following table summarizes the techniques of identifying the privacy information access behaviors:

Category of privacy check	Example of Android API calls
Telephony identifiers	Uses of APIs under the `TelephonyManager` will allow the application to read telephony services and state which may leak sensitive information, such as IMEI, SIM serial number, and cell ID. The examples of APIs (methods) under the `TelephonyManager` are `getCellLocation()`, `getDeviceId()`, `getLine1Number()`, `getNeworkOperator()`, `getSimSerialNumber()`.
Audio/video interception	There are two primary APIs used to do the audio and video recordings, which are all under the `MediaRecorder` class. The `setAudioSource` defines the audio sources for recording, and the `SetVideoSource` configures the source for video recording.
Suspicious backdoor connection	The class `ConnectivityManager` can be used to query the state of network connectivity. In addition, the uses of `WifiConfiguration.toString` can be an indicator of reading WiFi credentials. The use of `Socket` can be a potential backdoor connection to a remote IP address and port: • `ServerSocket` • `Connect` • `DatagramSocket`
Abuses of phone calls and SMS	The following may be an indicator of making phone call or SMS: • `Android.provider.Telephony.SMS_RECEIVED` (defined in `AndroidManifest.xml`) • `SmsManager.sendTextMessage` • `android.intent.action.CALL` • `android.intent.action.DIAL`
Data leakage	The privacy data on the phone can be contacts and SMS. The following APIs are indicators of reading the data: • `ContactsContract.CommonDataKinds` • `"content://sms/inbox"`
Root behaviors	The application is detecting the rooted device or super user privilege: • `superuser, supersu, noshufou` • `isDeviceRooted` • `/system/bin/su, /system/xbin/su` • `RootTools.isAccessGiven`

Privacy scanning with Androwarn

To automate the privacy scanning with APK, we can use the tool Androwarn which is a Python script to do the privacy information scanning.

Step 1 – scanning of an APK

The execution of Androwarn takes some parameters, such as the APK, the report format, the level of verbosity, and the lookup to Google Play. The Google Play lookup is recommended to be disabled if the testing environment can't connect to the internet, as follows:

```
$ python androwarn.py -i ./SampleApplication/bin/SampleApplication.apk -r
html -v 3 -n
```

For detailed usage of Androwarn, refer to python `androwarn.py -h`

Step 2 – review the report

If you have specified the HTML report output in the previous step, then the report will be generated under the `/androwarn/Report`, as follows:

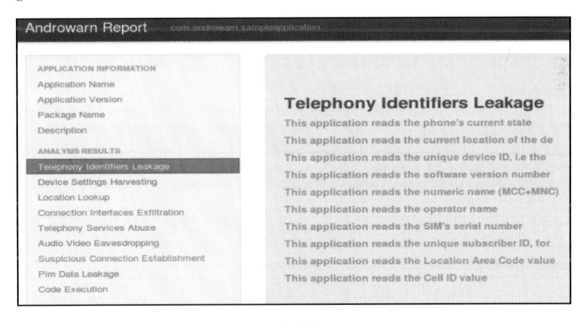

Information Leakage in Androwarn report

General process of APK security analysis

The security analysis of an Android application normally requires a certain reverse engineering process. The APK is a compressed file. The first step would be to get the APK uncompressed and reverse it into DEX bytecode or Smali resource files. These can be seen as Android intermediate resource files. Then, the DEX can further be reversed into Java class in order to get the Java source code. The following diagram shows the process and related tools we will demonstrate in the coming section:

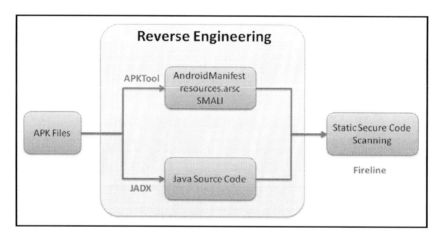

Reverse engineering of an APK

This is a list of the tools for the reverse engineering of APK and security analysis:

Tools	Usage in security testing
`apktool_2.1.0.jar`	The `APKTool` is used to reverse the APK file into Smali, resource files and also extract the `manifest.xml`
`JADX`	It's used to reverse the APK file into Java source code
`fireline_1.5.6.jar`	It's used to do static secure code scanning based on resource, and Java source codes
`goatdroid.apk`	It's the vulnerable sample APK

Here is how we place these tools in the folder for the purposes of the coming demonstration:

Folder structure of the testing environment
\jadx
\APKscan
+------ apktool_2.1.0.jar
+------- fireline_1.5.6.jar
+------- goatdroid.apk   /
+-------\JavaSource1
+-------\JavaSource2
+-------\Output

Step 1 – use APKTool to reverse the APK to Manifest.xml, Smali and resources

The purpose of this step is to generate the Smali, resource files, and manifest.xml for initial security analysis. There are some security issues that can be identified by these file types, such as sensitive information exposure and incorrect permission settings, as follows:

```
$ Java -jar apktool_2.1.0.jar  d  goatdroid.apk  -o  JavaSource1  -f
```

Step 2 – use JADX to reverse the APK into Java source code

This will reverse the APK into Java source code. Then, we can do static secure code scanning in the next setup, as follows:

```
$ Jadx  goatdroid.apk  -d  d:\JavaSource2
```

Step 3 – use Fireline to scan all the Java source files

Finally, we use Fireline to scan all the resource files, manifest and Java source code for security issue, as follows:

```
$ Java  -jar  fireline_1.5.6.jar  -s  d:\JavaSource  -r  d:\Output
```

Step 4 – review the scanning results

The scanning report of the Fireline will be generated under the d:\Output:

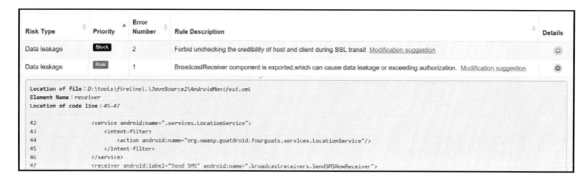

Fireline scanning report

Static secure code scanning with QARK

QARK (Quick Android Review Kit) is a Python security scanner to identify Android application vulnerabilities. QARK can take APK or Java as source input, and do the reverse engineering automatically for further security analysis. It's easy to install and use. We will be using the QARK to analyze the goatdroid.apk in the following steps.

Step 1 – install QARK

The installation can be easily done by python PIP, as follows:

```
$ pip install qark
```

Step 2 – APK scanning with QARK

To scan the APK, execute the python script qarkMain.py with parameters, as follows:

```
$ python qarkMain.py -p qark/sampleApp/goatdroid/goatdroid.apk    --source=1
```

For detailed usage of the qarkMain, refer to the python qarkMain.py -h.

Step 3 – review the results

The report will be generated under the `/qark/report/report.html`. The following screenshot shows the scanning report of the `goatdroid.apk`:

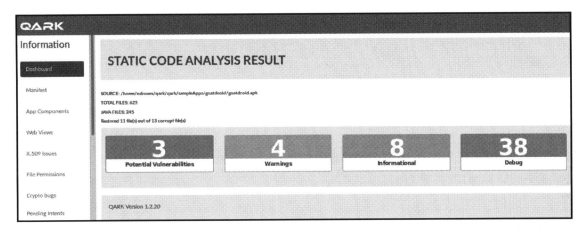

QARK scanning report

Automated security scanning with MobSF

The **mobile Security Framework** (**MobSF**) provides security analysis for the iOS, Windows, and Android applications. It can also do dynamic analysis based on runtime behaviors of the application. The MobSF provides an easy to use UI for users to drag and drop the mobile applications for analysis and also includes rest API interface to do further CI/CD integration with your automation framework. In our demonstration, we will show how to use MobSF API to analyze a sample vulnerable Android application, `goatdroid.apk`.

Step 1 – set up the MobSF

The easiest way to set up the MobSF is by using docker. The following setup will enable the MobSF running with `8000` port. Once the setup is ready, the MobSF management console can be visited by using a browser with the URL, `http://127.0.0.1:8000/`, as follows:

```
$ docker pull opensecurity/mobile-security-framework-mobsfdocker run -it -p
8000:8000 opensecurity/mobile-security-framework-mobsf:latest
```

Step 2 – upload the APK by REST API

In this step, we will use the REST `API` `/api/v1/upload` to upload the APK to the MobSF. For the value of the API Key, and usage of each rest API, refer to `http://localhost:8000/api_docs`. In our MobSF, the API key is `563d64fc5054d3b239ac0419f1d6b2378465f5c80e1778c283eb1e3265bdd7ae`:

```
$ curl -F 'file=@goatdroid.apk' http://localhost:8000/api/v1/upload -H
"Authorization:563d64fc5054d3b239ac0419f1d6b2378465f5c80e1778c283eb1e3265bd
d7ae"
```

To review if the upload is successful, you may use the browser to view the URL, `http://127.0.0.1:8000/recent_scans`.

Step 3 – scan the APK

To scan the APK, use the API `/api/v1/scan`. It needs to provide the following parameters, `file_name`, `MD5` hash value of the APK, and the API key:

```
$ curl -X POST --url http://localhost:8000/api/v1/scan --data
"scan_type=apk&file_name= goatdroid.apk&hash=
969bac4cb8392ceb79b5e60f310e480b" -H
"Authorization:563d64fc5054d3b239ac0419f1d6b2378465f5c80e1778c283eb1e3265bd
d7ae"
```

Step 4 – download the report

The API `api/v1/download_pdf` is used to generate a PDF file of the scanning results. It requires the MD5 hash value of the APK, and API key. We also specify the filename as `MobSFTest.pdf` in our example:

```
$ curl -X POST  --url  http://localhost:8000/api/v1/download_pdf  --data
"hash=969bac4cb8392ceb79b5e60f310e480b&scan_type=apk" -H
"Authorization:563d64fc5054d3b239ac0419f1d6b2378465f5c80e1778c283eb1e3265bd
d7ae"  >  MobSFTest.pdf
```

The following screenshot shows parts of the scanning report in `MobSFTest.pdf`:

Scanning report of MobSF

Summary

In this chapter, we introduced secure Android development practices, such as secure coding guidebook, security best practices, and the OWASP mobile security testing guide. Based on these secure implementation and testing practices, we also illustrated some automated scanning tools. The Fireline is used to scan the Java source code for security issues. The Androwarn is specific for privacy and sensitive information scan. The QARK and MobSF are the integrated Android security scan frameworks that can do the reverse of APK and secure code scanning.

We also illustrated the secure code review patterns for Android applications. There are some high-risk APIs that may result in serious security issues. We categorized the security issues into SQL injection, insecure SSL handling, command injection, webview XSS, insecure files I/O, and the insecure communication. In addition, we also listed the API calls that related to privacy, such as telephony identifiers, audio interception, potential backdoor connection, abuse of phone call, data leakage, and root behaviors.

To automate these security and privacy security reviews, we apply different tools based on the scenario. We use Fireline for the secure code scanning, but it will require the Java source code. Androwarn is used to do privacy scanning for any APK files. We used QARK to do the automated APK static security scanning. Finally, the MobSF is introduced for Windows, iOS, and Android applications security review. MobSF can also do the dynamic security scanning. The operations of MobSF can be automated by restful API was also demonstrated.

In the next chapter, we will discuss the infrastructure security for system hardening, secure communication and configurations.

Questions

1. Which one of the following is not for Android security?
    1. Fireline
    2. Androwarn
    3. QARK
    4. NMAP

2. Which of the following is not for the review of potential SQL injection?
    1. `execSQL`
    2. `NullHostnameVerifier`
    3. `sqlite`
    4. `database`

3. Which of the following is related for the SSL secure communication
    1. `setDefaultHostnameVerifier`
    2. `SSLCertificateSocketFactory`
    3. `ALLOW_ALL_HOST_VERIFIER`
    4. All of above

4. For the review of privacy information access, which Android API is not related to telephony identifiers?
    1. `getDeviceId`
    2. `getNeworkOperator`
    3. `setAudioSource`
    4. `getSimSerialNumber`

5. Which one of the tools can not do Android reverse engineering?
    1. APKTool
    2. JADX
    3. Fireline
    4. QARK

Further reading

- **Fireline Android static analysis**: `http://magic.360.cn/en/index.html`
- **Android privacy scan (Androwarn)**: `https://github.com/maaaaz/androwarn/`
- **Mobile Security Framework (MobSF)**: `https://github.com/MobSF/Mobile-Security-Framework-MobSF/wiki/1.-documentation`
- **Quick Android review kit**: `https://github.com/linkedin/qark/`
- **AndroBugs framework**: `https://github.com/AndroBugs/AndroBugs_Framework`
- **OWASP mobile testing guide**: `https://legacy.gitbook.com/book/sushi2k/the-owasp-mobile-security-testing-guide`
- **JADX**: `https://github.com/skylot/jadx`
- **DEX2JAR**: `https://github.com/pxb1988/dex2jar`
- **Android Cuckoo Sandbox**: `http://cuckoo-droid.readthedocs.io/en/latest/`
- **Vulnerable APK—GoatDroid.APK**: `https://github.com/linkedin/qark/blob/master/tests/goatdroid.apk`
- **Vulnerable APK—InSecureBankv2.APK**: `https://github.com/dineshshetty/Android-InsecureBankv2`
- **Android APK Scan**: `https://github.com/itsmenaga/apkscan/blob/master/apkscan.py`
- **Android Static Code Analyzer**: `https://github.com/vincentcox/StaCoAn`
- **Android Security 2017 Year in Review**: `https://source.android.com/security/reports/Google_Android_Security_2017_Report_Final.pdf`
- **Google App security improvement program**: `https://developer.android.com/google/play/asi`
- **Mobile Security Framework API docs**: `https://github.com/MobSF/Mobile-Security-Framework-MobSF/wiki/3.-REST-API-Documentation`

8
Infrastructure Security

The Android security was discussed in the previous chapter, and this chapter will focus on the infrastructure and platform security. For a PaaS platform or even SaaS service providers, the fundamental security requirement is to ensure that the infrastructure is secure. Therefore, the security operations team will need to do regular scanning on the infrastructure to ensure security configurations for security compliance. The infrastructure security includes the secure configuration with web services, database and OS, the secure communication protocol such as TLS v1.2, and the uses of secure versions of third-party components and dependencies. We will illustrate how to set up your own automated scanning framework to run these regular secure configuration inspections.

The topics to be covered in this chapter are as follows:

- The scope of infrastructure security
- Secure configuration best practices
- Network security assessments with Nmap
- CVE vulnerability scanning
- HTTPS security check with SSLyze
- Behavior driven security automation—Gauntlt

The scope of infrastructure security

The scope of infrastructure or platform security covers the operating system, virtualization, docker, web services, database, and secure communication.

The review of infrastructure security includes identifying the known vulnerable components, secure configurations, and secure communication protocols:

Infrastructure/platform security	Description	Open source tools and resources
Known vulnerable components	The known vulnerable CVE component is one of OWASP top 10 threats. If a component is exploited, the application can be vulnerable for remote injection or data leakage security risks.	• OpenVAS • NMAP • OWASP Dependency Check • RetireJS
Secure configuration	The secure configuration is to ensure the OS, Web, virtualization, and databases are configured securely such as password complexity, removal of default settings, or disable unnecessary services.	• OpenSCAP • CIS benchmarks • STIG
Insecure network communication	The followings secure communication protocol versions should be used: • SFTP instead of FTP • TLS 1.2 instead of HTTP, SSL, and TLS 1.1 • SNMP V3 instead of v1/v2 • SSH v2 instead of SSH v1 or Telnet	• NMAP • SSLyze

Secure configuration best practices

There are some industry security practices we can refer to for the secure configuration of the infrastructure. Here we will introduce three practices: the Center for Internet Security benchmarks, **Security Technical Implementation Guides** (**STIGs**), and the OpenSCAP Security Guide.

CIS (Center for Internet Security) benchmarks

The **Center for Internet Security (CIS)** benchmarks provides a wide range of secure configuration recommendations. It covers the following areas:

- Desktops and web browsers
- Mobile devices
- Network devices
- Security metrics
- Servers—operating systems
- Servers—other
- Virtualization platforms and cloud

In addition to providing secure configuration, the CIS also provides some tools for secure configuration scanning.

For information, refer to `https://learn.cisecurity.org/benchmarks`.

Security technical implementation guides (STIGs)

The STIGs provide more application-specific secure configuration suggestions. However, the STIG security guides are in XML format. To view the STIGs, you needs to download a STIG Viewer, which is a Java JAR. Follow the following steps to view the Ubuntu STIG:

1. Download the STIG Viewer from the URL. `https://iase.disa.mil/stigs/pages/stig-viewing-guidance.aspx`
2. Unzip the file and click the `STIGViewer-2.8.jar` to open the viewer
3. Download the Ubuntu STIG from the `https://iase.disa.mil/stigs/os/unix-linux/Pages/index.aspx`
4. Unzip to get the file, `U_Canonical_Ubuntu_16-04_LTS_STIG_V1R1_Manual-xccdf.xml`
5. Use the STIG Viewer to load the XML by the menu **File | Import STIG**

The following screenshot shows the results of importing the Ubuntu profile in the STIG Viewer:

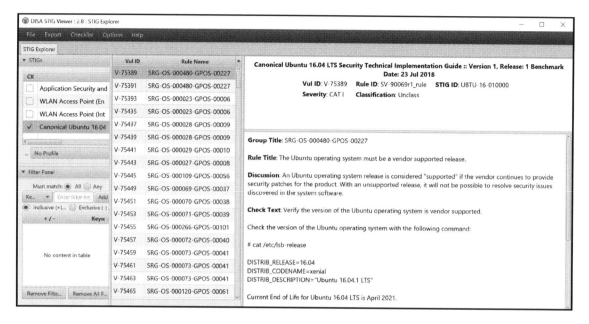

STIG viewer

OpenSCAP security guide

The OpenSCAP is mainly focused on OS secure configuration guides that can be found at `https://static.open-scap.org/`. In addition, OpenSCAP also provides several kinds of scanning tools to check the configurations, such as OpenSCAP Base, SCAP Workbench, and OpenSCAP Daemon. We will demonstrate the uses of SCAP Workbench in the following section:

SCAP Security Guides

for Fedora Linux
for Red Hat Enterprise Linux 7
for Red Hat Enterprise Linux 6
for Red Hat Enterprise OpenStack Platform 7
for CentOS 7
for CentOS 6
for Scientific Linux 7
for Scientific Linux 6
for Debian 8
for Ubuntu 14.04
for Ubuntu 16.04
for Wind River Linux
for Chromium
for Firefox
for Java Runtime Environment
for Webmin

SCAP security guides

Step 1 – installation of SCAP workbench

SCAP Workbench is one of secure configuration scanning tool that provides the GUI to do remote scanning. The SCAP Workbench tool can be downloaded here `https://github.com/OpenSCAP/scap-workbench/releases`.

In our demonstration, we download the Windows version MSI installer for remote SSH to scan target Linux secure configurations.

Step 2 – OpenSCAP security guide

Once the package MSI installer `scap-workbench-1.1.5-1.msi` is downloaded and installed, launch the `scap-workbench.exe`. It will ask you to load a security profile. We selected RHEL7 in our example. You may specify the SSH host to do the scanning.

The following screenshot shows how SCAP works:

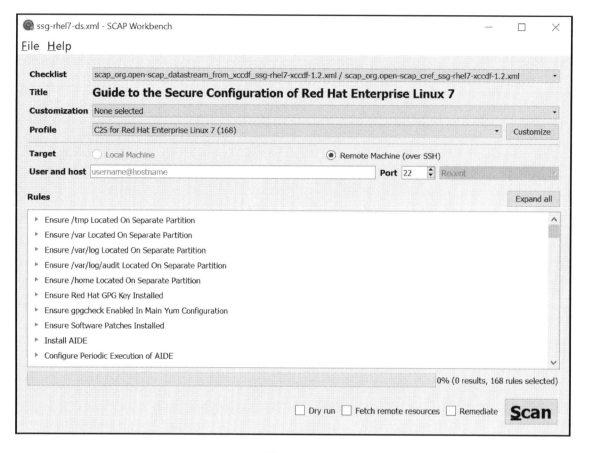

SCAP Workbench

Network security assessments with Nmap

Network Mapper (**Nmap**) is an open source network security scanning tool. It's widely used to do host, services, port system security audits, and also the SSL vulnerability. Identifying all the hosts, services, protocols, and communication ports on the network is the first step for network security assessment.

The installation of Nmap will depend on the OS.

The common network security assessment scenario and Nmap commands are listed in the following table:

Common network security assessments scenarios	Nmap command
Fast scan for listening ports	nmap -F --open -Pn
Scan for any missing HTTP security headers such as XSS-Protection	nmap -p80 --script http-security-headers -Pn
DOS attack with HTTPS Slowloris	nmap -p80,443 --script http-slowloris --max-parallelism 500 -Pn
Scanning for all TCP listening ports	nmap -p1-65535 --open-Pn
Scanning for all UDP listening ports	nmap -p1-65535 -sU --open-Pn
Scanning for common ports	Nmap -p21, 23,80, 137,138, 443, 445, 1433, 3306, 1521, 3389 --open pPn

Nmap usage tips

Nmap usage tips. To improve the scanning accuracy, here are some of the recommendations for the Nmap command execution:

- When the result is no-response, it may happen under the heavy load or high-delay network environment. If you are sure a specific port is listening but the result returns no-response. It's suggested to add the delay time by using -scan_delay <time>.
- If the scanning result is open|filtered, it can be concluded that the port is open or closed. It only means there may be proxy or firewall in between the target scan port.
- Nmap can be extended by using **Nmap Scripting Engine** (NSE) to do other security testing, such as SSL checks, XXS, and even SQL injection scans.

Nmap can also be extended to do CVE vulnerability scanning. For example, we can use the Vulscan module that enables Nmap to query offline vulnerability database after the service identification scanning.

In addition to Nmap, MASScan and ZMAP are alternative tools to consider. In terms of network port scanning, scanning with MASScan can have a quick result in a short time.

CVE vulnerability scanning

The known vulnerability scan is to identify the known CVE of the modules, libraries, source code, add-ons, services, and applications used in the infrastructure. To archive these kinds of scanning, we will introduce two main different approaches. The OWASP dependency check is a local scan of files to identify the vulnerabilities. This type of scan approach can be more accurate than a network scan. However, if the local scan of files is not feasible, we will use the network scan Nmap instead. Here is the summary of these two scan approaches:

	OWASP dependency check	NMAP-VulScan
Approaches	Package properties, such as libraries, filename	Network communications, such as port and protocol versions
Vulnerability database query	CVE, NVD Data Feeds	CVE, OSVDB, ExploitDB, and so on
Local/remote scan	A local scan of files and packages	Remote scan over the network

The following diagram shows two different scan approaches to identify known vulnerabilities. The **NMAP-VulScan** is using network scan approach and the OWASP dependency check is to scan local files properties:

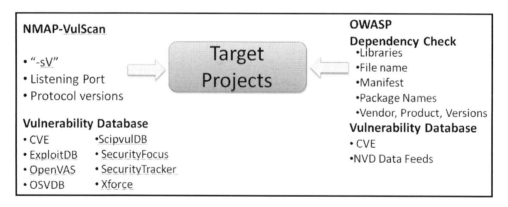

NMAP-VulScan and OWASP dependency check for vulnerabilities scan

Known vulnerable components scan by VulScan

Follow the following steps to install the NMAP VulScan and do the scanning.

Step 1 – installation of VulScan

The installation of VulScan is mainly the NMAP script file `vulscan.nse` and also other known vulnerable database CSV files. We may use git clone command to download all we need. Once these files are downloaded, copy those files to the installed Nmap folders, `Nmap\scripts\vulscan\*`:

```
git clone https://github.com/scipag/vulscan.git
```

Step 2 – NMAP scanning with VulScan

To do the NMAP scanning with the `vulscan.nse` script on the target `zero.webappsecurity.com`, we may execute the following command line:

```
$ nmap -sV --script==vulscan.nse zero.webappsecurity.com
```

Known vulnerable components scan by OWASP dependency check

Here we demonstrate the uses of the command line version of OWASP dependency check for local files scanning.

Step 1 – installation of OWASP dependency check

The OWASP dependency check provides JAR, which can be executed under command line. It also provides Marven, Gradle, and Jenkins plugins. In our example, to reduce any required dependencies, we will use the command-line version for the demonstration. Download the ZIP file and unzip it, as follows:

```
https://www.owasp.org/index.php/OWASP_Dependency_Check.
```

Step 2 – CVE scanning with OWASP dependency check

After unzipping the command line version, the BAT or SH to execute the dependency check will be under the following folder:

- `\dependency-check\bin\dependency-check.bat`
- `\dependency-check\bin\dependency-check.sh`

In our demonstration, we specify to scan the `d:\tools\Jmeter5`, and output the testing report under existing folder which will be `\dependency-check\bin`, as follows:

```
> dependency-check.bat   --project   Testing   --out   .   --scan
d:\tools\Jmeter5
```

For other uses of the command line, refer to `https://github.com/jeremylong/DependencyCheck`.

The following screenshot shows the execution results of executing the listed command:

```
D:\tools\dependency-check\bin>dependency-check.bat --project Testing --out . --scan d:\tools\Jmeter5
[INFO] Checking for updates
[INFO] starting getUpdatesNeeded() ...
[INFO] NVD CVE requires several updates; this could take a couple of minutes.
[INFO] Download Started for NVD CVE - 2003
[INFO] Download Started for NVD CVE - 2002
[INFO] Download Started for NVD CVE - 2004
[INFO] Download Started for NVD CVE - 2005
[INFO] Download Started for NVD CVE - 2007
[INFO] Download Started for NVD CVE - 2006
```

Dependency check execution

Once the scanning is done, you may find the `dependency-check-report.html` under the `\dependency-check\bin`.

Here is the sample of dependency check output HTML report:

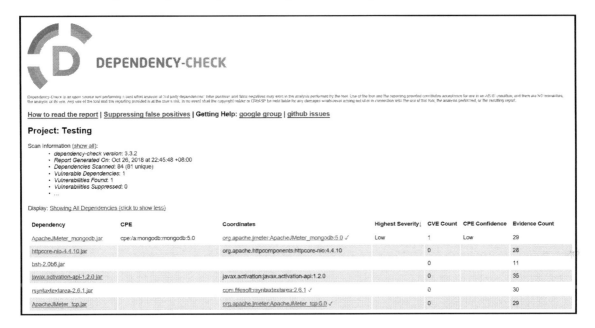

Dependency	CPE	Coordinates	Highest Severity	CVE Count	CPE Confidence	Evidence Count
ApacheJMeter_mongodb.jar	cpe:/a:mongodb:mongodb:5.0	org.apache.jmeter:ApacheJMeter_mongodb:5.0 ✓	Low	1	Low	29
httpcore-nio-4.4.10.jar		org.apache.httpcomponents:httpcore-nio:4.4.10		0		28
bsh-2.0b6.jar				0		11
javax.activation-api-1.2.0.jar		javax.activation:javax.activation-api:1.2.0		0		35
rsyntaxtextarea-2.6.1.jar		com.fifesoft:rsyntaxtextarea:2.6.1 ✓		0		30
ApacheJMeter_tcp.jar		org.apache.jmeter:ApacheJMeter_tcp:5.0 ✓		0		29

Dependency Check Report

> **TIP**
>
> In addition to security vulnerabilities issues, the uses of open source also need to pay attention to the license types and restrictions such as GPL or LGPL. The suggested open source tools that can do the license scanning are: Askalono, Licensee, LiD, and ScanCode.

HTTPS security check with SSLyze

It's common to apply HTTPS for web service security. The HTTPS requires proper security configuration to ensure secure communication. The common security issues can be weak cipher suites, insecure renegotiation, Heartbleed attack, invalid certificates, and insecure protocols, such as SSL v3, TLS 1.1. (TLS v1.3 is the latest secure communication protocol at the time of the writing.)

The following table lists common HTTPS security testing scenario and the uses of SSLyze:

HTTPS security testing scenarios	SSLyze command options
Check for Heartbleed vulnerability	`Sslyze --heartbleed`
Check for certificate validation	`Sslyze --certinfo=basic`
Check compression for CRIME attack	`Sslyze --compression`
Check for renegotiation issues	`Ssylze --reneg`

The SSLyze can be installed by Python PIP or there is also a Windows `.exe` version, which can be found at `https://github.com/nabla-c0d3/sslyze/releases`:

```
$ pip install --upgrade sslyze
```

To execute the SSLyze `.exe` under Windows, refer to the following command:

```
$ sslyze    --regular    demo.testfire.net
```

The `sslyze --help` will list the detailed usage of each command option:

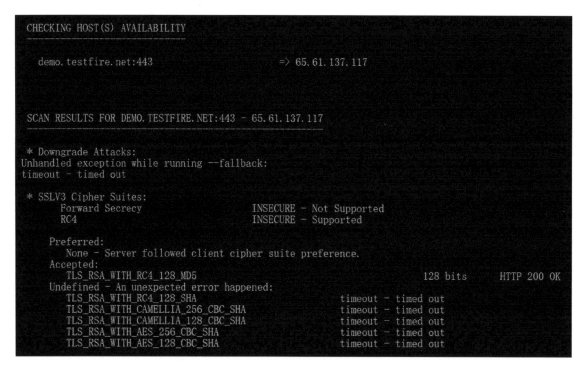

Sslyze scanning report

In addition to SSyze, the **Mozilla TLS Observatory** also provides a suite of tools to scan the TLS services. For an online version of TLS check, refer to `https://observatory.mozilla.org`.

Behavior-driven security automation – Gauntlt

The Gauntlt is a behavior-driven security testing framework. Behavior-driven means all the testing scripts are written in the following format. The purpose of the behavior-driven framework is to make the testing steps easier to understand. For a non-security team, the testing scripts and testing reports can be easily communicated for what and how security is tested:

```
Feature: Description for all scenarios in this file
 Scenario: Description of this scenario
 Given...
 When...
 Then...
 Scenario:...
```

Here is the Gauntlt testing scrip to trigger the NMAP scanning. In this scenario, we use NMAP to ensure the port 80 is listening:

```
Scenario: NMAP Scanning for website
 When I launch a nmap attack
 Then the output should contain:
  """
      80/tcp
  """
```

Step 1 – Gauntlt installation

The Gauntlt provides several ways of installation including Docker and Vagrant. You may also download the Gauntlt installation shell script to install the Gauntlt.

Follow the following steps to install the `gauntlt`:

```
$ git clone https://github.com/gauntlt/gauntlt
$ cd gauntlt
$ source ./install_gauntlt_deps.sh
$ bash ./ready_to_rumble.sh
$ gauntlt
```

Be reminded that the Gauntlt installation only includes the security tools adopters. The security tools such as Arachni, CURL, Nmap, sqlmap, and SSLyze will require additional installation respectively.

Step 2 – BDD security testing script

We will create a script file named `nmap.attack`. The key purpose of the script is to use NMAP to validate if the target website, ScanMe, is listening with the expected ports, such as 22, 25, 80, and 443. As you can see, the BDD-style script makes it easier for readers to understand the testing steps, the testing scenario, and the expected results:

Feature: nmap attacks for `scanme.nmap.org`
Background: It's used to check ScanMe website port listening status 22, 25, 80, and 443

Given nmap is installed
And the following profile:

```
| name          | value            |
| hostname      | scanme.nmap.org  |
| host          | scanme.nmap.org  |
| tcp_ping_ports | 22,25,80,443    |
```

Scenario: Verify server is open on the expected set of ports using the `nmap-fast` attack step
    When I launch a `nmap-fast` attack
    Then the output should match `/80.tcp\s+open/`

Step 3 – execution and results

Use the following command to execute the NMAP attack script:

```
$ gauntlt      nmap.attack
```

The following screenshot shows the execution result of the Gauntlt with NMAP script:

```
Feature: nmap attacks for scanme.nmap.org and to use

  Background:                    # nmap.attack:4
    Given "nmap" is installed  # gauntlt-1.0.13/lib/
    And the following profile: # gauntlt-1.0.13/lib/
      | name          | value              |
      | hostname      | scanme.nmap.org |
      | host          | scanme.nmap.org |
      | tcp_ping_ports | 22,25,80,443    |

  Scenario: Verify server is open on expected set of
Checking nmap-fast and nmap-fastRunning a nmap-fast
  This is a fast nmap scan that should run in 10 second
    When I launch a "nmap-fast" attack
.rb:12
    Then the output should match /80.tcp\s+open/

  Scenario: Verify server is open on expected set of
    When I launch an "nmap" attack with:
      """
      nmap -F <hostname>
      """
    Then the output should match:
      """
      80/tcp\s+open
      """
```

Gauntlt scanning results

In addition, there are also other examples of the execution of security tools. You may find the scripts under the `/gauntlt/examples/` folder. Taking SSLyze testing as an example, the script can be found under `/gauntlt/examples/sslyze/ssylze.attack` or at: `https://github.com/gauntlt/gauntlt/blob/master/examples/sslyze/sslyze.attack`:

```
$ gauntlt     sslyze.attack
```

If Gauntlt identifies the specified security tool, SSLyze, is not installed, it will also prompt proper guidance for the installation steps as the following screenshot shows:

```
Background:                    # sslyze.attack:3
  Given "sslyze" is installed # gauntlt-1.0.13/lib/gauntlt/attack_adapters/sslyze.rb:1
      sslyze.py not installed or $SSLYZE_PATH not set!

    1. Download sslyze from: https://github.com/iSECPartners/sslyze
    2. In your .zshrc or .bash_profile (or whatever), set $SSLYZE_PATH

       export SSLYZE_PATH=/path/to/sslyze.py

    3. Make sure you have python installed:

       $ which python
```

Gauntlt missing tools

Summary

In this chapter, we discussed the infrastructure security, which includes security scanning for known vulnerable components, secure configuration, and secure communication. For the secure configuration, the CIS benchmarks, STIGs, and the OpenSCAP security guide are the guidelines we can follow. For the vulnerable components scanning, we demonstrated two technical approaches. One is CVE scanning with NMAP network scanning and the other is file scanning with OWASP dependency check. For the secure communication, we introduced SSLyze for the HTTPS commutation settings. Finally, we also demonstrated one BDD automation framework Gauntlt to do the NMAP scanning.

In the next chapter, we will introduce more BDD automation frameworks to apply to security testing.

Questions

1. Which of the following is not used for known vulnerable components scanning?
   1. OpenVAS
   2. NMAP
   3. RetireJS
   4. SQLMap

2. Which of the following is not security guidelines for configurations?
   1. OpenSCAP
   2. STIG
   3. CVE
   4. CIS Benchmarks

3. If I'm looking for a specific product secure configuration, which of the following references are suggested?
   1. STIG
   2. OpenSCAP
   3. CIS Benchmarks
   4. NIST

4. What security assessment does NMAP do?
   1. Fast Scan for listening ports
   2. DOS attack with HTTPS Slowloris
   3. Scanning for all TCP listening ports
   4. All of above

5. Which of the following is a vulnerability database?
    1. CVE
    2. ExploitDB
    3. OSVDBE
    4. All of the above

6. Which of the following does SSLyze not do?
    1. Check for Heartbleed vulnerability
    2. Check for certificate validation
    3. Check for known CVE
    4. Check compression for CRIME attack

Further reading

- **Automate the secure configuration scanning with OpenSCAP**: `https://www.open-scap.org/tools/openscap-base/`
- **System Configuration Audit Tools (system, kernel, permissions, services, network, distro, and external)**: `https://github.com/trimstray/otseca`
- **RapidScan**: `https://github.com/skavngr/rapidscan/`
- **Nmap Reference Guide**: `https://nmap.org/book/man-briefoptions.html`
- **Mozilla SSL Configuration Generator**: `https://mozilla.github.io/server-side-tls/ssl-config-generator/`
- **OpenSCAP for security configuration scanning**: `https://www.open-scap.org/`
- **ZMAP network scanner**: `https://zmap.io/`
- **MASScan for quick port scanning**: `https://github.com/robertdavidgraham/masscan`
- **Advanced vulnerability scanning with Nmap NSE**: `https://github.com/scipag/vulscan`
- **Gauntlt BDD Security Testing Framework**: `https://github.com/gauntlt/gauntlt`
- **OWASP Dependency Track**: `https://dependencytrack.org/`
- **NMAP NSE (Nmap Scripting Engine)**: `https://nmap.org/nsedoc/`
- **Askalono License Texts Scan**: `https://github.com/amzn/askalono`

9

BDD Acceptance Security Testing

In this chapter, we will discuss the challenges of cross-team communication within a large software development team. The team who executed the security testing may understand what has been tested and how, but other non-technical teams such as product management, marketing, or even customers may not understand the context just from reading the testing reports. Therefore, we will introduce **behavior-driven development (BDD)** acceptance testing with automation security testing. BDD security testing is introduced to improve the communication of the nature of security testing to all functional teams involved. We will use security testing tools on top of the BDD security automation testing framework and hook into the testing process.

The following topics are to be covered in this chapter:

- Security testing communication
- Overview of BDD security testing
- BDD testing framework

Security testing communication

Being able to articulate the security testing plan, execution, and results in a way that non-security team members can understand is critical to the project. This will help stakeholders understand what security testing is performed and how. Too many technical and security domain-specific terms may result in the security testing being too difficult to understand.

For example, the business objective of security is to protect the application against injection attacks. However, in the domain of security testing, 'injection attacks' may be specifically described as **XML External Entity (XXE)** attacks, **Cross-Site Scripting (XSS)** attacks, command injection, and SQL injection. Use of this terminology may cause communication gaps and misunderstanding between security and non-security stakeholders.

The following table lists the security business objectives for general stakeholders and the corresponding security testing techniques for dealing with them:

Security business objective and scenario	Security testing techniques
Web scanning—Executing automated web application-level security testing to identify vulnerabilities in the web application	OWASP Top 10 security testing includes 10 common security issues such as injection, broken authentication, sensitive data exposure, XXE, broken access control, security misconfiguration, XSS, insecure deserialization, known vulnerabilities, and insufficient logging and monitoring.
Verifying that the **TLS/SSL (Transport Layer Security/Secure Sockets Layer)** configuration of the web server is secure	The testing of the SSL configuration does not only include the uses of secure protocols and a secure cipher suite, but also the following: • Tests for CCS injection vulnerability • Tests for renegotiation vulnerabilities • Tests for CRIME vulnerability • Tests for BREACH vulnerability • Tests for POODLE (SSL) vulnerability • Tests for FREAK vulnerability • Tests for BEAST vulnerability • Tests for LOGJAM vulnerability • Tests for DROWN vulnerability
Verifying that sensitive information is transmitted in a secure manner	• Secure communication with TLS v1.2 • Secure remote connection with SSH v2 instead of Telnet

What is BDD security testing?

ATDD stands for **Acceptance Test-Driven Development**, and BDD means behavior-driven development. In some scenarios, these two terms can be interchangeable. The purpose of adopting ATDD or BDD is to make security testing more transparent for all project members. The security testing results can provide quick feedback on the meeting of business objectives, for instance. The other purpose of BDD adoption is the provision of dynamic documentation for the whole project cycle, since BDD is done with an English-like language that follows the **Given, When, Then (GWT)** format.

In this book, we introduce the use of Robot Framework and Gauntlt to achieve BDD security automation testing. Here is a comparison of these two BDD testing frameworks:

	Robot Framework	**Gauntlt**
Type	ATDD	BDD
Script format	Keyword-driven script: • `Execute command` • `Create session` • `Should not contain`	Scenario-driven script: • Given... • When... • Then the output should...
Integration with security tools	No additional security adapters are needed. Robot Framework uses one of the following approaches to communicate with security tools: • **command-line interface (CLI)**: Execute command • REST API: Requests library	Gauntlt requires security adapters, although it provides a generic command-line adapter that can be used for most CLI security tools
Popularity	Robot Framework is a widely used automation testing framework, perhaps due to ease of use	Gauntlt may be new to both the automation and security testing teams

Adoption of Robot Framework with sqlmap

Let's take SQL injection testing as a simple example to see the effects of Robot Framework adoption. As the business objective, we would like to avoid any SQL injection attacks, which may result in authentication bypasses, information leakage, authorization bypasses, and command injection. Before integration with Robot Framework, SQL injection execution by `sqlmap` will be as follows:

```
$ python sqlmap.py   -u   "http://demo.testfire.net/"   -- batch   --
banner
```

The following is an excerpt from the `sqlmap` testing results. If these results were just delivered to stakeholders with no context, few stakeholders would be able to understand the report:

```
[xx:xx:39] [INFO] heuristic (basic) test shows that GET parameter 'id'
might be
injectable (possible DBMS: 'MySQL')
[xx:xx:39] [INFO] testing for SQL injection on GET parameter 'id'
[xx:xx:39] [INFO] testing 'MySQL >= 4.1 AND error-based - WHERE or HAVING
clause '
[xx:xx:39] [INFO] GET parameter 'id' is 'MySQL >= 4.1 AND error-based -
```

```
WHERE or
HAVING clause' injectable
GET parameter 'id' is vulnerable.
```

The following steps show how this is done.On the other hand, if we apply Robot Framework to execute `sqlmap`, the Robot Framework execution script would be much more understandable, as certain keywords are used to define the testing steps.

Step 1 – Robot Framework setup and preparation

Robot Framework is implemented with Python, and supported on both Python 2 and Python 3. The easiest way to install Robot Framework is by the Python PIP package:

```
$ python -m pip install robotframework
```

In addition, it's suggested to install the Robot Framework IDE, called RIDE, which will help to edit the testing script easier. RIDE can be installed by using PIP. Once the installation is done, RIDE can be started by running `ride.py`:

```
$ pip install robotframework-ride
```

Once the installation of RIDE is done, execute `ride.py` to launch it.

Once installation of Robot Framework is done, we may install `sqlmap` as follows:

```
$ git clone --depth 1 https://github.com/sqlmapproject/sqlmap.git sqlmap-dev
```

Step 2 – sqlmap with Robot Framework

The Robot Framework script for executing sqlmap is as follows:

```
*** Settings ***
Library SSHLibrary
*** Variables ***
${HOST_URL}                     http://demo.testfire.net
*** Test Cases ***
SQL Injection Testing
[Documentation]   Use SQLmap to do the SQL injection testing on target host
${output}=  Execute Command   python sqlmap.py -u ${HOST_URL} -- batch --
banner
Should  Not Contain    ${output}     vulnerable
```

In this case, we use `Execute Command`, and `Should Not Contain` to define the `sqlmap` execution steps and the expected testing results. Here you can see the difference that the adoption of Robot Framework makes. Robot Framework is a keyword-driven acceptance testing framework that is able to describe the testing steps with well-defined expected results.

Furthermore, Robot Framework is also flexible enough to define other user-defined keywords and variables, to make its output more understandable.

Testing framework – Robot Framework with ZAP

In `Chapter 8`, *Infrastructure Security*, we introduced the uses of Gauntlt, the BDD security framework. Here we will introduce another BDD automation testing framework, Robot Framework. The reason that we also introduce Robot Framework is that it's widely used in automation testing and also supports various kinds of testing frameworks, such as Selenium for web UI testing, and Requests for REST API testing. Its flexibility and simple keyword-driven script make Robot Framework a good fit for security testing automation. Robot Framework is a generic automation framework for acceptance testing and ATDD. We will use Robot Framework to manage the execution steps of ZAP. The typical web security scanning steps with ZAP are listed here:

1. Start a headless ZAP
2. Create a new ZAP session
3. Perform a spider scan
4. Perform an active scan
5. Review the scanning results and ZAP alerts

In the following steps, we will demonstrate one simple ZAP spider scan to understand how Robot Framework can be used to do security testing with OWASP ZAP.

Step 1 – environment setup and preparation

In this case, we will launch ZAP as proxy mode with the listening port `8090`. We will perform ZAP execution by using Robot Framework to send the REST API to ZAP. Refer to the previous section for the installation of Robot Framework.

In addition, we will also need the `requests` library to enable Robot Framework to send the HTTP requests to ZAP. The requests library can be installed as follows:

```
$ pip install -U   requests
$ pip install -U   robotframework-requests
```

Step 2 – the Robot Framework script for the ZAP spider scan

In this Robot Framework script, we will trigger ZAP to do the spider scan for the website. The following steps will be performed:

1. ZAP spider scan for the target website
2. Get the ZAP scanning response; the response status code should be 200 success

There are two main approaches to using Robot Framework for ZAP web scanning. The first one is using the OWASP ZAP CLI, which allows us to send commands to control ZAP executions. The other way is using the ZAP REST API. Since we have demonstrated how to execute via the command line in the previous sqlmap example, we will demonstrate how to use the ZAP REST API with Robot Framework. To achieve this, Robot Framework will need to install the Requests library to send the RESTful API requests to ZAP.

Here is the full Robot Framework testing script in plain text with the filename ZAP RequestsSample.robot:

```
*** Settings ***
Suite Teardown Delete All Sessions
Library Collections
Library String
Library RequestsLibrary
Library OperatingSystem
*** Variables ***
${url}                          http://demo.testfire.net
${SpiderScan}
http://localhost:8090/JSON/spider/action/scan/?zapapiformat=JSON&formMethod
=GET&url=${url}&maxChildren=&recurse=&contextName=&subtreeOnly=
*** Test Cases ***
```

```
ZAP Spider Scan
[Tags] get skip
Create Session                    ZAP
${SpiderScan}
${resp}=                                   Get Request              ZAP
/
Should Be Equal As Strings ${resp.status_code} 200
```

If you are using **RIDE** (**Robot Framework Test Data Editor**), here is the script in text mode:

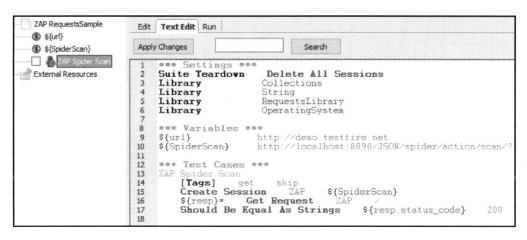

Text view of a ZAP spider scan in Robot Framework

Here is the table view of the script in RIDE:

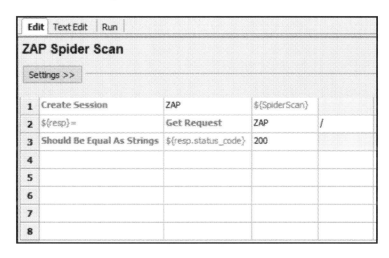

Table view of a ZAP spider scan in Robot Framework

Here are the required settings in RIDE:

ZAP Requests Sample

Source	c:\Python27\Scripts\myRobot\ZAP RequestsSample.robot

Settings >>

Import	Name / Path	Arguments	Comment
Library	Collections		
Library	String		
Library	RequestsLibrary		
Library	OperatingSystem		

Variable	Value		Comment
${url}	http://demo.testfire.net		
${SpiderScan}	http://localhost:8090/JSON/spider/action/scan/?zapapiformat...		

ZAP settings in Robot Framework

Once the spider scan is done, the web security scanning results will be found at the following URL:

```
$
http://localhost:8090/HTML/core/view/alertsSummary/?zapapiformat=HTML&formM
ethod=GET
```

Alternatively, use the ZAP CLI to output the report in HTML as follows. Be reminded that the ZAP CLI will need to be installed with `pip install zapcli`:

```
$ zap-cli report -o  ZAP_Report.html  -f html
```

It's always recommended to use RIDE to edit the Robot Framework script although the script can also be edited by using notepad. In RIDE, you may mouse move over the keyword and press CTRL to present the detailed usage.

Step 3 – robot script execution

Execute the following commands under the CLI console:

```
$ robot    "ZAP RequestsSample.robot"
```

Once the execution is done, the Robot Framework testing report will be generated under the same folder of the robot script. `output.xml`, `log.html`, and `report.html` will be generated.

Summary

In this chapter, we mainly discussed how to apply a BDD framework to security testing. The security testing process and results can be difficult to understand for a non-security team; the adoption of a BDD security framework can reduce the communication gap. For example, a security team may test for POODLE vulnerability; in business language, that would be the verification of the secure communication of TLS.

We introduced two automation frameworks, Robot Framework and Gauntlt. Robot Framework uses a keyword-driven approach to define the testing steps and Gauntlt uses a GWT approach to define the testing scripts. We demonstrated the testing of SQL injection by using `sqlmap`, and illustrated how Robot Framework can be used to execute `sqlmap`. In the Robot Framework script, we use `Execute Command` to execute `sqlmap`, and we define the expected results by using `Should Not Contain`.

We also illustrated how to integrate Robot Framework with ZAP. We mainly use the Robot Framework Requests library to send restful APIs to OWASP ZAP. In the Robot Framework script, we defined a custom variable, SpiderScan, to execute the spider scan restful API in OWASP ZAP.

After learning about Robot Framework integration with `sqlmap` and ZAP, we will begin a project to practice all previously mentioned techniques and tools in the coming chapters.

Questions

1. Which one of these is not the main purpose of BDD framework adoption?
   1. Communication with non-security stakeholders
   2. Defining testing script in business language
   3. Using the GWT structure to define script
   4. Reducing testing script development time

2. What is used in Robot Framework to execute sqlmap?
   1. SSHLibrary
   2. Execute Command
   3. Should Not Contain
   4. All of the above

3. What's the correct order of ZAP execution?
   1. Active Scan → Spider Scan → Review results
   2. Spider scan → Active Scan → Review Results
   3. Active Scan → Quick Scan → Review Alerts
   4. Quick Scan → Active Scan → Spider Scan

4. What Robot Framework library do we use to execute a ZAP RESTful API?
   1. Collections
   2. The Requests library
   3. String
   4. Operating system

5. Where we can define a custom variable in Robot Framework?
   1. Settings
   2. Variables
   3. Test cases
   4. None of above

Further reading

- **Robot Framework user guide**: `http://robotframework.org/robotframework/latest/RobotFrameworkUserGuide.html`
- **OWASP ZAP web security testing**: `https://github.com/zaproxy/zaproxy`
- **Robot Framework ZAP library**: `https://github.com/airesv/robotframework-zaplibrary`
- **Robot Framework Requests library**: `https://github.com/bulkan/robotframework-requests/#readme`
- **Robot Framework Security Testing Modules**: `https://github.com/we45`
- **OWASP ZAP CLI**: `https://github.com/Grunny/zap-cli`

10
Project Background and Automation Approach

In this chapter, we will introduce a project and security objective to do with automated security to work on in the coming chapters. We will also further explore the considerations that need to be made when it comes to security and automation framework selection. Some tools are good for specific security testing but may have shortcomings when it comes to automation framework integration. Finally, we will set up all the necessary environments for the coming security automation practices.

This chapter will mainly focus on the following:

- Considerations for security and automation framework selection
- Setup of a security and automation environment

Case study – introduction and security objective

In this case study, we will discuss a software service delivery team. The team regularly releases web services and mobile applications. The security objective is to ensure that there are no major security vulnerability issues before each service or mobile application goes live. We will use the following vulnerable demo projects:

- **For web services**: OWASP NodeGoat and OWASP WebGoat
- **For mobile services**: Vulnerable APK by MobSF

The NodeGoat project comprises an online *RetireEasy* Employee Retirement Savings Management service. The website includes several major OWASP Top 10 vulnerabilities, and we will apply several automation testing tools and techniques to identify those security issues in the coming chapters. In this book, we focus on how to build an entire security automation testing framework, rather than just identifying security issues and exploring the details of each security issue.

For the OWASP NodeGoat web service, you may use the online version (`http://nodegoat.`
`herokuapp.com/`) or install it from the NodeGoat source on GitHub.

Selecting security and automation testing tools

There are some key considerations to bear in mind when selecting security automation tools. The tools you select may depend on the integration of your existing automation testing framework. In our case, the testing framework and tools we will use are Python, Selenium, Robot Framework, and Jenkins. We also plan to use DefectDojo to present the results of those tools. In summary, the key considerations that we should bear in mind when selecting our security and automation frameworks are as follows:

- **Is it open source?** If so, that would provide the flexibility to extend or customize the frameworks.
- **Is it cross-platform?** The frameworks must be able to work in Windows or Linux.
- **What interfaces are there?** The GUI interface may easy to use but it can be a barrier to automation. We will also look for tools that support **command-line interfaces (CLIs)** or RESTful API interfaces for further integration.
- **What is the report format?** This will depend on how we integrate and consolidate testing reports. The XML and JSON report formats are widely used; we may consider whether the tool can generate such report formats.

The security tools listed in the following table meet these criteria and will also be used in coming chapters through case studies.

Please refer to the *Further reading* section for references to each security tool:

Open source security testing tools	Details
Arachni Scanner	• Web security scanner • CLI integration • JSON report format to import into DefectDojo
Dependency check	• CLI for vulnerable dependency components • XML format
Nmap	• CLI for network security scanning • XML output
Retire.js	• CLI for vulnerable JavaScript scanning • JSON format
Visual Code Grepper (VCG)	• Secure code scanning based on patterns • CSV or XML formats
SSLLabs-Scan	• CLI to scan the vulnerability of the SSL configuration
ZAP	• CLI for web security scanning • XML format
Mobile Security Framework or **Quick Android Review Kit (QARK)**	• Python scripts for static Android security analysis

Automated security testing frameworks

A typical automated security testing framework may include the following key components:

Key components	Usage scenarios
Security testing tools	Security testing tools are in charge of testing for specific security vulnerabilities, such as **cross-site scripting** (**XSS**) and SQL injection, and also analyze HTTP responses for security issues
Target web service	In our example, we will use NodeGoat and WebGoat for the target testing website
Testing results analysis	Security testing tools may provide initial testing reports. Testing results can be further integrated by either a testing framework, such as Robot Framework, or a testing management tool, such as ArcherySec or OWASP DefectDojo
Robot Framework	This is a popular automation testing framework that we can use to integrate an automation process
Automation scripts	These scripts can be Python, Java, shell, or Robot Framework scripts for executing, handling data, or interpreting results
Security payloads	It's used as data input for the security testing. For example, the HTTP requests can be sent with the security payloads to test XSS or SQL injection attacks. FuzzDB and SecList are common sources of security payloads.

The following diagram shows an example of what a security automation testing framework might look like:

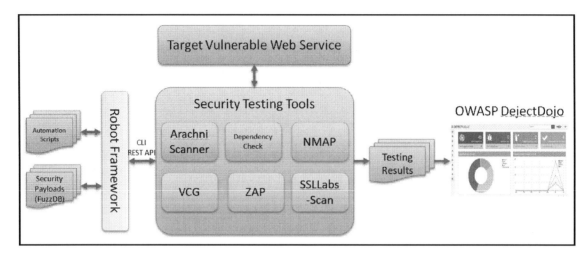

Example of a security automation testing framework

Environment and tool setup

The following table lists tools, environments, and their descriptions. Please also refer to the *Further reading* section for the relevant references:

Environment and tools	Usage and references
Vulnerable website	This will be the OWASP NodeGoat project, which is a vulnerable web project written in Node.js For the online version, go here: `http://nodegoat.herokuapp.com/` For the offline version. go here: `https://github.com/OWASP/NodeGoat`
WebGoat	This is an OWASP vulnerable project in Java
ZAP-CLI	This is used to operate OWASP ZAP in console mode
ZAP	This is an OWASP web security scanner
OWASP DefectDojo	DefectDojo is a security tool that automates application security vulnerability management and provides security findings and metrics in a web-based dashboard
Robot Framework	This is an **Acceptance Test-Driven Development** (**ATDD**) automation testing framework
Selenium	This is a web UI testing framework

SeleniumBase	This is a wrapper of Selenium. It's written in Python and makes Selenium scripts simpler
Gauntlt	This is a **behavior-driven development** (**BDD**) testing framework for security testing
Nmap	This is a network scanner
JMeter	This is used to send HTTP requests and monitor HTTP responses in this book
Serpico	`https://github.com/SerpicoProject/Serpico/releases`
RapidScan	This is used to trigger several security testing tools and output the results in the console
sslScan	This is used to scan vulnerable protocols of SSL communication
wfuzz	This is for the fuzz testing of HTTP requests
FuzzDB	This is the security payloads fuzz database
Retire.js	This is used to scan the vulnerable libraries for JavaScript

Summary

In this chapter, we introduced our security testing project, NodeGoat. We also discussed the security tool selection criteria we should consider when building a security automation framework. A security automation framework typically includes security testing tools, a web service, testing results, an automation framework (such as Robot Framework), automation scripts, and security payloads. In coming chapters, we will learn how to complete the testing automation framework and demonstrate automated testing for the NodeGoat website, fuzz API security testing, and infrastructure security testing.

Questions

1. For automation, what kinds of interface can suffice?
    1. CLI
    2. RESTful API
    3. Python library
    4. All of the above

2. Which one of these is not a key component of the typical security automation framework?
    1. Automation scripts
    2. Security payloads
    3. Security testing tools
    4. Virtualization

3. What is QARK used for?
   1. Android security analysis
   2. Web security scanning
   3. SSL vulnerabilities scanning
   4. Known CVE scanning

4. Which one of these is used for a known vulnerability scan?
   1. Dependency check
   2. Retire.js
   3. Nmap
   4. All of the above

5. Which one of these is a key consideration of the automation framework?
   1. Report format
   2. Cross platform
   3. Integration interface
   4. All of the above

Further reading

- **NodeGoat**: https://github.com/OWASP/NodeGoat
- **NodeGoat tutorials**: https://nodegoat.herokuapp.com/tutorial
- **Arachni Scanner**: http://www.arachni-scanner.com/
- **Dependency check**: https://www.owasp.org/index.php/OWASP_Dependency_Check
- **Nmap**: https://nmap.org/
- **Retire.js**: https://retirejs.github.io/retire.js/
- **VCG**: https://github.com/nccgroup/VCG
- **SSLLabs-Scan**: https://github.com/ssllabs/ssllabs-scan
- **ZAP**: https://github.com/zaproxy/zaproxy
- **Mobile Security Framework**: https://github.com/MobSF/Mobile-Security-Framework-MobSF
- **QARK**: https://github.com/linkedin/qark/
- **OWASP DefectDojo**: https://defectdojo.readthedocs.io
- **Robot Framework**: http://robotframework.org/

11
Automated Testing for Web Applications

In this chapter, we will use three case studies to learn different security automation techniques for use against the vulnerable NodeGoat site. The first case is to automate OWASP ZAP by using the ZAP-CLI, which will help identify any initial security issues on the website before authentication. In the second case, we will be using selenium to do the user sign-in, in order to access some authenticated pages and identify more potential security issues. In the final case, we will use JMeter to do the sign-in with external CSV data and detect potential command injection security issues.

The topics that will be covered in this chapter are as follows:

- Web security automation testing with OWASP ZAP using the CLI
- Web security automation testing with ZAP and Selenium
- Web security testing with ZAP, JMeter, and DDT with FuzzDB

Case 1 – web security scanning with ZAP-CLI

In this small NodeGoat web security testing scenario, we will automate OWASP ZAP by using the ZAP-CLI for security smoke testing. The ZAP-CLI provides a quick scan, which is handy because it achieves the following in one command:

- Open a URL to the target website
- Spider scan to discover web resources (URLs) extensively on the target website
- Active scan to identify more potential security issues by using known attacks

We will perform the following steps to execute the ZAP-CLI and review the security results by

Step 1 – installation of ZAP-CLI

Assuming you have installed OWASP ZAP, the installation of the ZAP-CLI can be easily done with this command:

```
$ pip install --upgrade zapcli
```

To ensure the success of the ZAP-CLI installation, you may try this command with help options:

```
$ zap-cli quick-scan --help
```

Step 2 – ZAP quick scan using the ZAP-CLI

To do a ZAP-CLI quick scan with specified XSS and SQL injection security policies, the following command can be used. The ZAP-CLI may require the API Key of ZAP. To access or disable the API Key, configure the **Disable the API Key** checkbox under the OWASP UI menu, **Tools** | **Options...** | **API**:

```
$ zap-cli quick-scan -s xss,sqli --spider -r http://nodegoat.herokuapp.com/
```

It will take a while for ZAP to finish the spider and active scan.

Step 3 – generate a report

There are a few ways we can generate an OWASP ZAP report. The first is to use alerts to show a summary list of the security issues:

```
$ zap-cli alerts
```

Furthermore, we can also use report to generate a detailed HTML or XML report. The XML report can be used to import into other security reporting tools, which we will introduce in Chapter 15, *Summary of Automation Security Testing Tips*:

```
$ zap-cli report -o   ZAP_Report.html   -f html
```

To generate the XML format report, execute this command:

```
$ zap-cli report -o ZAP_Report.xml -f xml
```

Uses of ZAP-CLI or ZAP RESTful API to automate the OWASP ZAP scan? The ZAP RESTful API is provided by default in ZAP, while the ZAP-CLI will require to install `zapcli`. If you only need basic web scan operations, the ZAP-CLI may fit your needs. However, if you need more control over ZAP, the ZAP RESTful API will be recommended.

Case 2 – web security testing with ZAP & Selenium

In this case for the security testing of NodeSign signin, we will be using a Selenium script to automate the following UI steps and OWASP ZAP will be running as a proxy mode to monitor and analyze all security issues based on HTTP requests/responses. We will do the sign-in with a valid username and password, then visit every authenticated page without further data input and updates. The purpose of this testing is to do a security smoke test of every authenticated page.

Here are the UI steps automated by Selenium:

- Visit the sign-in page: `http://nodegoat.herokuapp.com/login`
- Sign in with username = `user1` and password = `User1_123`
- Visit the contributions page after sign-in
- Visit the allocation page
- Visit the memos page
- Visit the profile

Follow the following instructions to proceed the testing.

Step 1 – Selenium Python script

We will create the Selenium Python script `NodeGoat_SigIn.py`. For those who are not familiar with Python, the script can be automatically generated by using Selenium IDE recorders such as Kantu or the Katalon recorder. These are browser extensions and can be downloaded from the web store. The Selenium script will launch the Firefox browser. Please ensure the Firefox web driver (geckodriver) is installed, which can be found here: `https://github.com/mozilla/geckodriver/releases`.

Please also refer to Chapter 13, *Automated Infrastructure Security*, for how to apply **data-driven testing (DDT)** in a Selenium script.

This sample code shows a Selenium/Python script used to log in to NodeGoat with user1/user1_123 credentials:

```
# -*- coding: utf-8 -*-
# NodeGoat_SignIn.py
from selenium import webdriver
from selenium.webdriver.common.by import By
from selenium.webdriver.common.keys import Keys
from selenium.webdriver.support.ui import Select
from selenium.common.exceptions import NoSuchElementException
from selenium.common.exceptions import NoAlertPresentException
import unittest, time, re

class SignIn(unittest.TestCase):
    def setUp(self):
        self.driver = webdriver.Firefox()
        self.driver.implicitly_wait(30)
    def test_sign_in(self):
        driver = self.driver
        driver.get("http://nodegoat.herokuapp.com/login")
        driver.find_element_by_id("userName").clear()
        driver.find_element_by_id("userName").send_keys("user1")
        driver.find_element_by_id("password").clear()
        driver.find_element_by_id("password").send_keys("User1_123")
        driver.find_element_by_xpath("//button[@type='submit']").click()
        driver.get("http://nodegoat.herokuapp.com/contributions")
        driver.find_element_by_xpath("//button[@type='submit']").click()
        driver.get("http://nodegoat.herokuapp.com/contributions")
        driver.get("http://nodegoat.herokuapp.com/allocations/2")
        driver.get("http://nodegoat.herokuapp.com/memos")
        driver.get("http://nodegoat.herokuapp.com/profile")
    def tearDown(self):
        self.driver.quit()


if __name__ == "__main__":
    unittest.main()
```

Step 2 – running ZAP as a proxy

In Chapter 5, *Security API and Fuzz Testing*, and Chapter 6, *Web Application Security Testing*, we introduced the installation and use of ZAP. Here, we will only discuss how to launch the browser with the Selenium script and the specified ZAP proxy, which is 127.0.0.1:8090 in our case.

Approach 1 – configure the system proxy

This approach may be the easiest way to achieve the result we want. If it's Windows, the system configuration can be done by IE proxy setting. If it's Linux, refer to the Linux network configuration to configure the proxy as 127.0.0.1:8090.

Approach 2 – Selenium Profile

In this approach, we define the selenium script to use the specified proxy as 127.0.0.1:8090. This will require a certain modification of the selenium script. Here is the sample script, which shows how to define the browser proxy. The self.driver = webdriver.Firefox() will need additional profile preference settings, as shown in this example:

```
# "Selenium Proxy Sample.py"
from selenium import webdriver

# Replace the 'self.driver = webdriver.Firefox()' with the following
profile = webdriver.FirefoxProfile()
profile.set_preference('network.proxy_type',1)
profile.set_preference('network.proxy.http',"127.0.0.1")
profile.set_preference('network.proxy.http_port',"8090")
driver=webdriver.Firefox(profile)
# End of Replacement


driver.get('http://nodegoat.herokuapp.com/login')
driver.close()
```

Approach 3 – using SeleniumBASE

If the script is done by using SeleniumBASE, the browser proxy can be specified with proxy command options. Please be aware that our example, `NodeGoat_SignIn.py`, cannot be executed directly by using SeleniumBASE. Here are the steps to convert our original selenium script into SeleniumBASE style. The steps work under the assumption that SeleniumBASE is installed, which can be done with `pip install seleniumbase`:

```
seleniumbase    convert    NodeGoat_SignIn.py
```

Then, we may execute the command with the proxy `127.0.0.1:8090`: The previous command will generate `NodeGoat_SignIn_SB.py`:

```
pytest "NodeGoat_SignIn_SB.py" --proxy=127.0.0.1:8090
```

When the testing is stable, it's suggested to execute the selenium testing script in headless mode. It means the testing will proceed without launching a real browser. It will simulate the execution in memory. This will improve the testing stability and cycle. For the uses of SeleniumBASE, specify the headless option, for example, `pytest my_test.py --headless --browser=chrome`.

Step 3 – generate ZAP report

The ZAP security testing report can be generated by one of the followings:

```
$ CURL "http://127.0.0.1:8090/OTHER/core/other/htmlreport/?formMethod=GET"
> ZAP_Report.HTML
```

Alternatively, if the ZAP-CLI is installed, the HTML report can be generated with this command:

```
$ zap-cli report -o   ZAP_Report.html  -f html
```

Case 3 – fuzz XSS and SQLi testing with JMeter

In *Case 3*, we will demonstrate the same user flows as in *Case 2*. The key difference in *Case 3* is that we will have the data input with SQL injection payloads. This will be done by using Jmeter with FuzzDB and CSV Config elements. In `Chapter 13`, *Automated Infrastructure Security*, we will also demonstrate how to do fuzz SQLi testing with selenium and Robot Framework.

Testing scenarios

After user sign-in, particularly in step 6, we will be using JMeter to send HTTP requests with FuzzDB security loads through the OWASP ZAP proxy to the target testing website, NodeGoat.

The testing steps are as follows:

1. Sign in to NodeGoat with the username `User1` and password `User1_123`
2. Visit the contributions page
3. Visit the allocations page
4. Visit the memos page
5. Visit the profile page
6. **Input the security payloads for SQL and command injection testing on the profile update page**
7. Log out
8. Generate the security reports in OWASP ZAP

During these steps, OWASP ZAP will be used to analyze the HTTP request/response traffic to identify potential security issues. The general steps to complete the automation testing will be as follows:

1. Set up the ZAP Proxy on port `8090` and JMeter
2. Define the JMeter scripts
3. Launch JMeter in the CLI with ZAP Proxy
4. Generate the ZAP report with the CLI
5. Shut down ZAP

Step 1 – prepare environment

To prepare the environment for this security testing scenario, we will mainly need JMeter, ZAP, and FuzzDB. This table lists the tools with the usage scenario in this security testing:

Tools	Usage scenario in security testing
JMeter	JMeter will be used to send HTTP requests with injection security payloads.
ZAP	ZAP will be running in proxy mode on port 8090, and will analyze security issues with the HTTP traffic.
FuzzDB	We will use the FuzzDB command injection payloads for the JMeter. Refer to this for the attack payloads: `https://github.com/fuzzdb-project/fuzzdb/tree/master/attack`.

Step 2 – define the JMeter scripts

Using JMeter can be very complex. In our case, we will only use parts of the necessary elements to complete the testing scenario. This table lists the use of JMeter elements in our case and also the configuration needed in each element:

JMeter elements	Usage and scenarios
HTTP Cookie Manager	It's used to maintain the authenticated cookie session after sign-in.
HTTP Header Manager	It's used to simulate browser behaviors with HTTP headers. We will apply the Chrome HTTP header in our case.
View Results	It's to review every HTTP request and response.
Response Assertion	The `Response Assertion` is included in every HTTP request to validate the HTTP request gets the expected HTTP response.
HTTP Request	It's used to send HTTP GET/POST requests to the target website.
CSV Data Set Config	It's used to read values from a CSV file.

We will create a JMeter Script with the following configurations, and save the script as `NodeGoat.jmx`:

JMeter elements	Configuration
HTTP Cookie Manager	No need to do any configuration.
HTTP Header Manager	Headers Stored in the Header Manager Name: Referer / User-Agent / Accept / Accept-Encoding / Cache-Control / Upgrade-Insecure-Requests Value: http://nodegoat.herokuapp.com/dashboard / Mozilla/5.0 (Windows NT 10.0; Win64; x64) AppleWebKit/537.36 (KHTML, like Gecko) Chrome/70.0.3538.110 Safari/537.36 / text/html,application/xhtml+xml,application/xml;q=0.9,image/webp,image/apng,*/*;q=0.8 / gzip, deflate / max-age=0 / 1
View Results Tree	No need to do any configuration.

HTTP Request - NodeGoat Sign	HTTP Request Method: POST Path: /login ☐ Redirect Automatically ☑ Follow Redirects ☑ Use KeepAlive ☐ Use multipart/form-data ☐ Browser-compatible headers Parameters Body Data Files Upload Send Parameters With the Request: <table><tr><td>Name:</td><td>Value</td><td>URL Encode?</td></tr><tr><td>userName</td><td>user1</td><td></td></tr><tr><td>password</td><td>User1_123</td><td></td></tr><tr><td>_csrf</td><td></td><td></td></tr></table>
Response Assertion	Fields to test: Text response Patterns to test: Employee retirement savings management
HTTP Request – contributions	HTTP Request Name: HTTP Request - contributions Comments: Basic Advanced Web Server Protocol [http]: http Server Name or IP: nodegoat.herokuapp.com HTTP Request Method: GET Path: /contributions ☐ Redirect Automatically ☑ Follow Redirects ☑ Use KeepAlive ☐ Use multipart/form-data ☐ B
Response Assertion	Field to test: Text response Patterns to test: Employee pre-tax
HTTP Request - Allocations	HTTP Request Name: HTTP Request - Allocations Comments: Basic Advanced Web Server Protocol [http]: http Server Name or IP: nodegoat.herokuapp.com HTTP Request Method: GET Path: /allocations/2
Response Assertion	Field to test: Text response Patterns to test: Stock performance
HTTP Request - Memos	HTTP Request Name: HTTP Request - Memos Comments: Basic Advanced Web Server Protocol [http]: Server Name or IP: nodegoat.herokuapp.com HTTP Request Method: GET Path: /memos
Response Assertion	Field to test: Text response Patterns to test: Send a memo
HTTP Request - Profile	HTTP Request Name: HTTP Request - Profile Comments: Basic Advanced Web Server Protocol [http]: http Server Name or IP: nodegoat.herokuapp.com HTTP Request Method: GET Path: /profile ☐ Redirect Automatically ☑ Follow Redirects ☑ Use KeepAlive ☐ Use multipart/form-data ☐ Browser-compatible headers
Response Assertion	Field to test: Text response Patterns to test: My profile

HTTP Request - Profile Update	
Response Assertion	Field to test: Text response Patterns to test: Profile updated successfully
HTTP Request – Logout	
Response Assertion	Field to test: Text response Patterns to test: New user?

Step 3 – prepare security payloads

From the sources of FuzzDB, we will prepare two files `cmdi.csv` for the data input of profile update. In the JMeter script, **CSV Data Set Config** will be added with the following configuration:

- **Filename**: `cmdi.csv`
- **Variable Names (comma-delimited)**: `cmdi`

This screenshot shows the JMeter script with **CSV Data Set Config**:

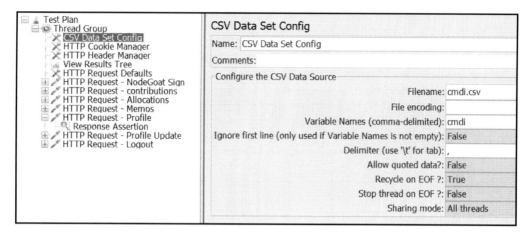

CSV Data Set Config for Command Injection in JMeter

Then, we can use the `${cmdi}` variable in **HTTP Request - Profile Update**. For example, we replace the value of **firstName** and **lastName** with `${cmdi}` to do command injection testing:

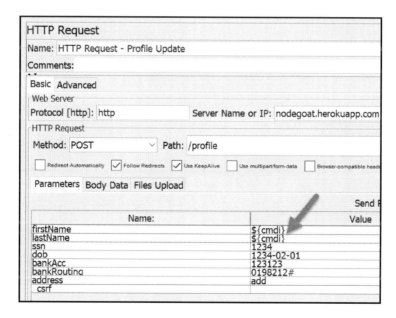

HTTP Request for Command Injection Testing in JMeter

To do the loop and read all the variables in `cmdi.csv`, we still need to change the **Loop Count** settings in **Thread Group**. For example, we will do the loop 10 times with each value in the `cmdi.csv`:

- **Loop Count**: 10

Step 4 – launch JMeter in CLI with ZAP proxy

To launch JMeter in console mode, we will specify the proxy to OWASP ZAP by using the –H:

```
$ jmeter    -n   -H   localhost -P   8090   -t    NodeGoat.jmx    -l
NodeGoat_result.jtl  -j  NodeGoat_result.log
```

In addition, the proxy settings of JMeter can also be configured by using **HTTP Request Defaults** under the **Advanced** tab.

Step 5 – generate a ZAP report

The ZAP security testing report can be generated by one of the followings:

```
$ CURL "http://127.0.0.1:8090/OTHER/core/other/htmlreport/?formMethod=GET"
> ZAP_Report.HTML
```

Should I select Selenium or JMeter as our security automation framework? Both tools can achieve similar testing results. Selenium simulates user behaviors in a real browser, but it may produce unexpected errors during UI testing. On the other hand, JMeter only sends HTTP requests and verifies HTTP responses, without rendering the UI in a browser. In addition, for the selection of tools, we may also consider integration with existing security or automation frameworks. For example, if the team has built all the automation based on JMeter, then JMeter may be a better choice for security automation.

Summary

In this chapter, we have demonstrated three technical approaches to NodeGoat security automation testing. The first approach is to use the ZAP-CLI to do a quick scan of the target website. This kind of testing can be used as a smoke test for every release. It helps us to identify potentially serious security issues. We also applied Selenium and JMeter to guide ZAP for authenticated pages and other web UI flows. Selenium can launch the browser to simulate a user's web operation behavior. JMeter sends the HTTP requests and asserts the HTTP responses for the API-level user sign-in flow.

For the selenium approach, it's suggested to use the Selenium IDE to record the sign-in operations and export to a Python unit test script. Once the script is generated, we execute the Selenium script with the OWASP ZAP proxy to identify the security issues.

For the adoption of JMeter, **CSV Data Set Config** is used to read all the values from a CSV file. **HTTP Cookie Manager** is applied to manage the authenticated session. **HTTP Request** is used to send HTTP POST/GET requests to the website. Then, the JMeter script is executed in CLI mode with specified the proxy to OWASP ZAP.

In Chapter 12, *Automated Fuzz API Security Testing*, we will focus on fuzz API automation testing.

Questions

1. What does Quick Scan do in OWASP ZAP?
    1. Opens a URL to the target website
    2. Spider scan
    3. Active scan
    4. All of the above
2. What element is used in JMeter to read a CSV file?
    1. CSV Data Set Config
    2. HTTP Cookie Manager
    3. HTTP Header Manager
    4. None of the above

3. Which element is used to maintain the sign-in session in Jmeter?
    1. HTTP Cookie Manager
    2. HTTP Header Manager
    3. HTTP Request
    4. Response Assertion

4. What are the benefits of integration ZAP with JMeter and selenium?
    1. To allow ZAP to scan authenticated web resources
    2. To control the security payloads with FuzzDB
    3. To simulate a normal user web operation
    4. All of the above

5. Which one is not correct about Selenium?
    1. Selenium will launch a browser for testing
    2. A Selenium script can also be executed without a browser in headless mode
    3. Selenium testing will require the specific web driver for the target browser
    4. All of the above are correct

Further reading

- **SeleniumBase**: https://github.com/seleniumbase/SeleniumBase
- **JMeter**: https://jmeter.apache.org
- **Selenium**: https://www.seleniumhq.org
- **Robot Framework**: http://robotframework.org

12
Automated Fuzz API Security Testing

API fuzz testing can be one of the most effective and efficient methods for both security and automation testing. API fuzz testing involves generating fuzz data as data input, sending HTTP requests with fuzz data, and analyzing the HTTP response for security issues. We will demonstrate several API fuzz automation tools (Wfuzz and 0d1n), fuzz techniques, and integration with automation testing frameworks (Selenium and Robot Framework DDT) in this chapter.

The topics that will be covered here are as follows:

- Fuzz testing and data
- API fuzz testing with automation frameworks (Wfuzz, 0d1n Selenium DDT, and Robot Framework DDT)

Fuzz testing and data

FuzzDB, Seclist, and Big List of Naughty Strings are data input sources for security fuzz testing. Here, we will introduce how to dynamically generate your own security payloads for fuzz testing based on needs. Fuzz testing is a testing technique used to explore unexpected data input that can cause potential security issues such as buffer overflows, unhandled exceptions, or data injection attacks. Fuzz testing requires a massive systematic random data input, called a fuzz, to test the target application in an attempt to make it crash or go out of service.

The following diagram shows the relationship between the fuzz data, testing tools, and ZAP in web security. We will demonstrate the uses of Radamsa to generate testing data, and illustrate how to apply **data-driven testing** (**DDT**) techniques and testing tools to send fuzz data for web security testing. OWASP ZAP plays the HTTP traffic security analysis proxy role between the testing tools and the web:

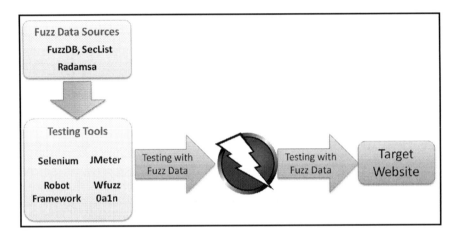

Fuzz Data, Testing Tools and ZAP

We will introduce open-source **Radamsa**, which generates fuzz data based on a user-defined data format. Follow these steps to learn how to use Radamsa.

Step 1 – installing Radamsa

For the Windows version, the tool can be downloaded here: `https://github.com/vah13/radamsa/releases`.

For the Linux version, refer to the following:

```
$ git clone  https://gitlab.com/akihe/radamsa
$ cd radamsa
$ make
$ sudo make install
$ radamsa --help
```

Step 2 – generating the Security Random Payloads

Here are some examples of data generation based on a given data sample:

- Generating email-format fuzz data:

```
$ echo "abc@test.com" | radamsa -n 5 --patterns od
```

- Generating SQL injection-related fuzz data:

```
$ echo "' or 1=1" | radamsa -n 5 --patterns od
```

- Generating JavaScript injection data:

```
$ echo "<script>alert(1)</script>" | radamsa -n 5 --patterns od
```

- Generating the XXX-XXX-XXXX format-based fuzz data:

```
$ echo "154-541-3214" | radamsa -n 5 --patterns od
```

- Generating date-format fuzz data:

```
$ echo "1977-12-01" | radamsa -n 5 --patterns od
```

The use of Radamsa enables us to dynamically generate fuzz data based on a sample input. Then, we can use that generated fuzz data as data input sources for further security testing.

Should I use FuzzDB or Radamsa? FuzzDB provides security data payloads for various kinds of security testing, such as SQL injection, XXE, XSS, and command injection. It's recommended you use FuzzDB for security testing. On the other hand, we use Radamsa to generate formatted data to test unexpected behaviors such as username, ID, telephone number, address, and date.

API fuzz testing with Automation Frameworks

In Chapter 5, *Security API and Fuzz Testing*, we demonstrated how to use JMeter to do fuzz testing with OWASP ZAP. In this chapter, we will demonstrate other techniques using Selenium/ **data-driven testing (DDT)** and the 0d1n. There is no one solution that fits all testing scenarios. It may depend on the skill-sets of the team, existing testing frameworks, and integration flexibility.

Some key considerations and applied scenarios are listed in this table:

Considerations	Applied scenarios and suggested technical approaches
Launch a browser	There are pros and cons to launching a browser for Web UI E2E automation. The key advantage is that it simulates the human behavior for complete E2E testing. However, this kind of testing execution cycle can be time-consuming and prone to error due to Web UI interactions. Both Selenium and Robot Framework support Web UI E2E automation. These two are very common automation testing frameworks.
Programming	Selenium supports a wide range of programming languages such as Java, Python, C#, and Ruby. During implementation, we suggest using the Selenium IDE to generate the related code and do further customization. The Robot Framework is keyword-driven. Although it doesn't require much programming skill, the team has to know how to use keywords and related libraries correctly. JMeter doesn't require programming, but it will require you to understand the HTTP GET/POST API requests of the target website. This can be done by using browser *F12* to monitor the http traffic. Then, we will define the HTTP requests in JMeter based on this information. 0d1n is a CLI tool. It doesn't require any programming, but you will need to understand the HTTP GET/POST API and the parameters of the target website.
Quick testing	0d1n and Wfuzz are standalone tools that can do a quick fuzz test on the target website without any dependencies. Although ZAP can also do fuzz testing, it currently can only be executed in GUI mode.
API-based testing	Jmeter, 0d1n, and Wfuzz are good candidates for HTTP API-level testing due to their simplicity of deployment and execution.
Authenticated pages	If the testing scenario requires authenticated pages to walk through, it's recommended to use JMeter, Selenium, and Robot Framework since these testing frameworks can do web UI testing very well.

The following table lists the key characteristics of various technical approaches to implementing fuzz testing:

	OWASP ZAP	JMeter	Selenium DDT	Robot Framework DDT	0d1n	Wfuzz
Dependency	No	OWASP ZAP	OWASP ZAP	CSVLibrary	OWASP ZAP	No
Coding	No	No	Yes, but the Selenium IDE can help to generate the script	No	No	No
Fuzz data handing	ZAP UI mode only	CSV Config in JMeter	DDT library in Python	CSV Library for Loop	Λ in the command line	FUZZ or FUZ2Z keyword
Testing report	Refer to OWASP ZAP	Refer to OWASP ZAP	Refer to OWASP ZAP	Refer to OWASP ZAP	Refer to OWASP ZAP	Output to the console or file
Fuzz multiple parameters	Yes	Yes	Yes	Yes	Yes, but other values may be filled as empty	Yes FUZZ, FUZ2Z, FUZ3Z..
Integration interface	No	RESTful APIs JMeter scripts	Selenium scripts	Robot Framework scripts	**command-line interface (CLI)**	CLI
Testing framework popularity	The API and CLI don't support fuzz testing at this point	High JMeter is common in REST API and performance testing	High Common web UI framework	High Common acceptance testing framework	Low 0d1n is specifically built for fuzz testing in the CLI	MED
Launch browser during testing	No	No	Yes	Yes	No	No

In the following sections, we will demonstrate how these techniques and tools can be applied to security fuzz testing with the NodeGoat sign-in API.

 Which is the best solution? If your team has created the automation frameworks you're using or you are familiar with specific tools such as JMeter, Selenium, or Robot Framwork, it's suggested you build on top of it instead of introducing a new one.

Approach 1 – security fuzz testing with Wfuzz

In this demonstration, we will use Wfuzz to do username and password fuzz testing with the sign-in page. The values of the username and password will be provided with `cmdi.csv` and `sqli.csv`.

Step 1 – installing Wfuzz

It's suggested you install Wfuzz on Linux. Follow these commands to install Wfuzz:

```
$ git clone https://github.com/xmendez/wfuzz
$ cd wfuzz/
$ sudo python setup.py install
```

Step 2– fuzz testing with sign-in

The basic use of Wfuzz testing with sign-in is shown as follows:

```
wfuzz -c -z file,name.csv -z file,pass.csv -f Wfuzz_report.html,html -d
"userName=FUZZ&password=FUZ2Z&_csrf=" http://nodegoat.herokuapp.com/login
```

Here is the explanation of how each option is used in our case:

Options	Explanation of use
`-c`	Color output on the console
`-z file,<filename>`	Read the values from a file to replace `FUZZ, FUZ2Z...FUZnZ`. In our example, we have two parameters to be replaced with fuzz data.
`-f <Output_filename>,html`	Output the result to an HTML file named `Wfuzz_report.html`
`-d "name=FUZZ"`	It defines the `POST` message body. The `FUZZ` keyword and `FUZ2Z` will be replaced with the file input, which was defined by using `-z file` previously.

Although it's not a must, it's also suggested to configure OWASP ZAP as a system proxy. This will allow OWASP ZAP to analyze the HTTP requests/responses for potential security issues. After all, OWASP ZAP includes a more powerful security detection engine while Wfuzz can only do basic results analysis.

Step 3 – reviewing the Wfuzz report

Wfuzz will output a summary report to the console and also in HTML. In the console, the response column shows the response code. It also shows the number of lines, words, and chars of the HTTP response, based on each specified Payload. Here are some tips for reading the HTTP response, based on this kind of fuzz testing:

HTTP response code	What it means in security testing
200	It means the target resource is available. It's useful for directory traversal to identify whether the resources, URL, or path are available.
302	If it's for sign-in testing, it can be an indicator of login success. If we are doing brute-force sign-in testing, we will be looking for the major variation responses among all the HTTP responses. For example, all other requests return 200, but a few requests return 302.
404	Page or resource not found. It's used to identify that the target resource is available.
401 or 403	This can be an indicator that the resource is available but the request is unauthorized.
50x	This can be a serious security issue; one of the following needs further investigation: • Excessive system information exposure • Symptoms of SQL injection due to error exposure • Denial of service

Here is a screenshot of the Wfuzz console output. Look for any variations in the responses. In this case, all of the responses are 200. If any requests return non-200 responses, they will need further investigation. For lines, words, and chars, we are also looking for a major variation of the request, which can be an indicator of potential security issue:

```
Target: http://nodegoat.herokuapp.com/login
Total requests: 8

=========================================================================
ID      Response   Lines       Word         Chars         Payload
=========================================================================

000007:  C=200      180 L       519 W        7570 Ch       "| ls - pass1"
000008:  C=200      180 L       519 W        7570 Ch       "| ls - pass2"
000004:  C=200      180 L       522 W        7576 Ch       "' or 1 = 1 - pass2"
000001:  C=200      180 L       518 W        7575 Ch       "username1 - pass1"
000002:  C=200      180 L       518 W        7575 Ch       "username1 - pass2"
000003:  C=200      180 L       522 W        7576 Ch       "' or 1 = 1 - pass1"
000005:  C=200      180 L       518 W        7570 Ch       "pass - pass1"
000006:  C=200      180 L       518 W        7570 Ch       "pass - pass2"

Total time: 4.792974
Processed Requests: 8
Filtered Requests: 0
Requests/sec.: 1.669109
```

In addition, Wfuzz also provides a HTML report. If you found any request suspicious, click **send POST** to trigger the HTTP request again:

Wfuzz testing report

Approach 2 – security fuzz testing with 0d1n

In this demonstration, we will be using another fuzz tool, 0d1n, to do fuzz testing with NodGoat sign-in.

Step 1 – installation of 0d1n

The installation of 0d1n requires it to be compiled from the source code and `libcurl` installed. Follow these commands shown as follows:

```
$ git clone https://github.com/CoolerVoid/0d1n/
$ sudo apt-get install libcurl-dev

$ sudo yum install libcurl-devel

$ make

$ ./0d1n
```

If the installation is successful, the `./0d1n` command should be able to list the detailed usage of the tool.

This screenshot shows the execution of `./0d1n` for the usage examples:

```
example 1 to find SQL-injection:
./0d1n --host 'http://site.com/view/1^/product/^/' --payloads payloads/sqli_list.txt --find_string_list sqli_str2find
_list.txt --log log1337 --tamper randcase --threads 5 --timeout 3 --save_response

example 2 to Bruteforce in simple auth:
./0d1n --host 'http://site.com/auth.py' --post 'user=admin&password=^' --payloads payloads/wordlist.txt --log log007
--threads 10 --timeout 3

example 3 to search XSS and pass anti-csrf token:
./0d1n --host https://page/test.php --post 'csrf={token}&pass=^' --payloads payloads/xss.txt --find_string_list paylo
ads/xss.txt --token_url https://page/test.php --token_name name_token_field --log logtest --save_response
notes:
Look the character '^', is lexical char to change to payload list lines...
Coded by Cooler
 coolerlair[at]gmail[dot]com
```

0d10 usage

Step 2 – execution of 0d1n with OWASP ZAP

The following command will trigger fuzz testing against the NodeGoat login page. In addition, 0d1n can also easily define the proxy which we will specify OWASP ZAP here. Although running ZAP can be optional, it will be a supplement to 0d1n to detect security issue based on HTTP requests/responses:

```
$ ./0d1n --host 'http://nodegoat.herokuapp.com/login' --post
'userName=user1&password=^&_csrf=' --payloads ./payloads/user.txt --log
log001 --threads 3 --timeout 5 --proxy 127.0.0.1:8090 --find_string_list
./payloads/response.txt --save_response --tamper randcase
```

Following are the list of commands used in execution of 0d1n:

Command options	Explanation of use
--host '<target Host>'	Define the target website
--post '<Post Message body>'	Define the POST message body. The ∧ symbol will be replaced with fuzz data, which is defined by payloads.
--payloads <filename>	Define the source of the payloads for fuzz data input
--log <logName>	The log name
--proxy <host:port>	In our case, we still use ZAP as a proxy to monitor security issues
--find_string_list <response.txt>	0d1n allows us to search for some suspicious strings in the HTTP response
--save_response	Enable the save response highlights view when you click on a HTTP status code in data tables
--tamper randcase	Use lowercase and uppercase random position in a string

Step 3 – review the ZAP report (optional)

To review the security issues identified by OWASP ZAP, execute this command:

```
$ zap-cli report -o   ZAP_Report.html  -f html
```

Approach 3 – Selenium DDT (data-driven testing)

In this approach, we will be using selenium to do the sign-in and the DDT techniques to read all the fuzz data from the file (sqli.csv).

Step 1: Selenium script with DDT

Here is the fuzz data we prepared for the username and password input. The `sqli.csv` file defined two columns of data, which are username and password:

```
username,password
a,a
)%20or%20('x'='x,''
%20or%201=1,' 1=1
```

The key highlight of the `SignIn_DDT_NodeGoat.py` Selenium Python script is the adoption of the DDT module. The code in bold is mostly related how to read each value from `sqli.csv` and replace them with the username and password parameters for every HTTP request:

```python
# -*- coding: utf-8 -*-
# SignIn_DDT_NodeGoat.py
from selenium import webdriver
from selenium.webdriver.common.by import By
from selenium.webdriver.common.keys import Keys
from selenium.webdriver.support.ui import Select
from ddt import ddt, data, unpack
import csv
import unittest, time, re

@ddt
class NodeGoatSignIn(unittest.TestCase):
    # the method is used to read the "sqli.csv" file.
    def get_csv_data(csv_path):
        rows = []
        csv_data = open(str(csv_path), "rb")
        content = csv.reader(csv_data)
        next(content, None)
        for row in content:
            rows.append(row)
        return rows
    @classmethod
    def setUp(self):
        self.driver = webdriver.Firefox()
        self.driver.implicitly_wait(30)

    # The @data and @unpack will help to read all the data in the 'sqli.csv'
    # for the testing loop of the test_sign_in method
    @data(*get_csv_data("sqli.csv"))
    @unpack
    def test_sign_in(self, username, password):
        driver = self.driver
```

```
        # The following steps may be changed based on your web UI
operations senarios.
        # Selenium IDE is suggested to generate the following scripts.
        driver.get("http://nodegoat.herokuapp.com/login")
        driver.find_element_by_id("userName").click()
        driver.find_element_by_id("userName").clear()
        driver.find_element_by_id("userName").send_keys(username)
        driver.find_element_by_id("password").click()
        driver.find_element_by_id("password").clear()
        driver.find_element_by_id("password").send_keys(password)
        driver.find_element_by_xpath("//button[@type='submit']").click()
    @classmethod
    def tearDown(self):
        self.driver.quit()
if __name__ == "__main__":
    unittest.main()
```

 The Selenium/Python script can be automatically generated by using the Katalon Recorder browser extension. Once the script is generated, add the DDT parts of the code shown in bold.

Step 2 – executing the Selenium script

If the SeleniumBASE framework is installed, we can use the following command to trigger test execution. The `127.0.0.1:8090` proxy is the OWASP ZAP proxy. By executing the command, it will launch Firefox for sign-in with every value defined in `sqli.csv`. It may take a while, since it will launch and close Firefox for every request:

```
$ pytest   SignIn_DDT_NodeGoat.py  --proxy=127.0.0.1:8090
```

Step 3 – review the ZAP report

Once the testing is done, refer to the OWASP ZAP report:

```
$ zap-cli report -o   ZAP_Report.html  -f html
```

Approach 4 – Robot Framework DDT testing

In this case, we will be doing the same scenario. However, instead of using Selenium and Python, we will use Robot Framework to perform the DDT testing for the NodeGoat sign-in. We will still read the `sqli.csv` file to do the username and password fuzz testing.

Step 1– Robot Framework environment setup

The Robot Framework environment setup may refer to Chapter 9, *BDD Acceptance Security Testing*. In this testing scenario, in addition to Robot Framework, we will also require the following external libraries:

Robot Framework library	How to install	Usage scenarios in this case
CSVLibrary	`pip install -U robotframework-csvlibrary`	Read values from the CSV file
SeleniumLibrary	`pip install --upgrade robotframework-seleniumlibrary`	Launch the browser and execute the defined web UI operations

In addition, the selenium web drivers also need to be installed on the testing machine. This approach assumes that ZAP is running and the system proxy is configured to the ZAP proxy properly.

Step 3 – Robot Framework script

To complete the testing scenario, here are some major robot framework keywords used in this case:

Keyword commands	Use of the keyword
read .csv file to list	Read the `sqli.csv` CSV file to the list
Open Browser	Open the browser
Log	Print the value to the log
FOR .....IN	This is a loop to read all the values of the CSV files
Input Text	Locate the NodeGoat sign-in username and password, and input the text with the values from `sqli.csv`
Click button	Click the **Submit** button on the NodeGoat website
Close Browser	Close the browser for every test

The Robot Framework `RF_DDT.robot` script will be defined as follows:

```
*** Settings ***
Library Collections
Library CSVLibrary
Library SeleniumLibrary
Library OperatingSystem
Library String
Library Collections

*** Test Cases ***
```

```
SignIn_DDT
Open Browser http://nodegoat.herokuapp.com/login
@{data}= read csv file to list sqli.csv
Log ${data}
:FOR ${x} IN @{data}
\ Log ${x}
\ Input Text id=userName ${x[${0}]}
\ Input Text id=password ${x[${1}]}
\ Click Button xpath=//button[@type='submit']
\ Log ${x[${0}]}
\ Log ${x[${1}]}
Close Browser
```

In the Robot Framework RIDE, the script will look like this. This screenshot shows the **Settings** section of the script:

Robot Framework settings

The screenshot shows the steps definition of the Robot Framework in the RIDE editor:

1	Open Browser	http://nodegoat.herokuapp.com/lc		
2	@{data}=	read csv file to list	sqli.csv	
3	Log	${data}		
4	:FOR	${x}	IN	@{data}
5		Log	${x}	
6		Input Text	id=userName	${x[${0}]}
7		Input Text	id=password	${x[${1}]}
8		Click Button	xpath=//button[@type='submit']	
9		Log	${x[${0}]}	
10		Log	${x[${1}]}	
11	Close Browser			

DDT Testing Script in Robot Framework

To execute the robot Framework execute the following command:

```
$ robot    RF_DDT.robot
```

The Robot Framework itself has limited capability to analyze security issues in HTTP responses. Therefore, it's suggested to configure OWASP ZAP as the system proxy.

Step 4 – review the ZAP report

Use this command to generate the ZAP report:

```
$ zap-cli report -o    ZAP_Report.html   -f html
```

Summary

In this chapter, we discussed various kinds of techniques to achieve API fuzz security testing. We have introduced the use of FuzzDB and seclist for the sources of data input. In addition, we also demonstrated the use of Radamsa, which allows us to dynamically generate fuzz data based on a specified data sample.

For the API fuzz testing, we also demonstrated some automation frameworks and tools such as JMeter, Selenium/DDT, Robot Framework DDT, 0d1n, Wfuzz, and integration with ZAP. During API fuzz testing, it's recommended to apply ZAP as a proxy to identify security issues. We demonstrated four different technical approaches.

Approach 1 is to do the testing using Wfuzz. It can do the fuzz testing with multiple parameters, and output a summary of response codes and the number of lines, words, and chars of every HTTP response. Wfuzz testing is a good candidate for login brute-force, directory traversal, and RESTful API testing.

In *Approach 2*, we use 0d1n for fuzz testing, which is similar to Wfuzz. During testing, we specified `find_string_list` and executed OWASP ZAP to identify security issues based on HTTP responses.

Selenium with DDT is demonstrated in *Approach 3*. The behavior is mostly close to human behaviors due to the launch of browser and Web UI interaction behaviors. In the selenium script, we apply a DDT module to read the FuzzDB files for the input of username and password. OWASP ZAP is used to identify security issues.

In the final approach, Robot Framework DDT is used. This is similar to the Selenium/DDT approach. However, the Robot Framework script is defined by keyword driven instead of programming languages. It makes the Robot Framework script more readable. In Robot Framework, CSVLibrary is used to read the CSV files for FuzzDB data input.

In the next chapter, we will introduce infrastructure security testing.

Questions

1. Which one is not used for fuzz testing a data source?
    1. FuzzDB
    2. Seclist
    3. Radamsa
    4. None of the above

2. Which automation framework cannot simulate human behaviors for web UI operations?
    1. Selenium
    2. Robot Framework
    3. ZAP
    4. All of the above

3. What is the keyword used for Wfuzz to replace with fuzz data in the command?
    1. FUZZ
    2. @
    3. ^
    4. DATA

4. Which one best describes the HTTP response code 401/403?
    1. URL or path is available
    2. An indicator of login success
    3. An indicator that the resource is available but the request is unauthorized
    4. Symptoms of SQL injection due to error exposure

5. What is not the key characteristics to use Robot Framework?
    1. Keyword-driven script
    2. SeleniumLibrary can be used to launch a browser and simulate human web operations
    3. Fast execution cycle
    4. CSVLibrary is used to read fuzz data files

Further reading

- **Naughty Strings**: https://github.com/minimaxir/big-list-of-naughty-strings/blob/master/blns.tx
- **FuzzDB**: https://github.com/fuzzdb-project/fuzzdb
- **Data Production System**: https://code.google.com/archive/p/ouspg/wikis/Blab.wiki
- **Robot Framework Selenium Library**: http://robotframework.org/SeleniumLibrary/
- **Robot Framework CSV Library**: http://github.com/s4int/robotframework-CSVLibrary
- **Wfuzz**: http://wfuzz.readthedocs.io/en/latest/
- **0d1n fuzz testing**: http://github.com/CoolerVoid/0d1n

13
Automated Infrastructure Security

In this chapter, we will demonstrate how to automate infrastructure security testing against the NodeGoat website. The infrastructure security testing will include known vulnerable JavaScript libraries, insecure SSL configurations, and the advanced NMAP NSE script testing technique for web security. At the end, we will also illustrate how to apply the BDD automation framework to SSLScan and NMAP.

The topics that will be covered in this chapter are as follows:

- Scan For known JavaScript vulnerabilities
- Scanning with OWASP dependency check
- Secure communication scan with SSLScan
- NMAP security scan with the BDD framework

Scan For known JavaScript vulnerabilities

JavaScript libraries are widely used in any website, and are also considered the most vulnerable components. As *Using Components with Known Vulnerabilities* is one of the OWASP Top 10 security issues, we will need to constantly monitor any major known vulnerable components on the web. In this demonstration, we will introduce how to scan for known vulnerabilities in JavaScript libraries.

We will be using RetireJS because it's simple to use and provides several ways of scanning, such as a command-line scanner, Grunt plugin, browser (Chrome/Firefox) extension, and also the Burp and OWASP Zap plugins. In our demonstration, we will be using the command-line scanner in the following steps.

Step 1 – install RetireJS

The installation of RetireJS requires us to use `npm`:

```
$ npm install -g retire
```

Step 2 – scan with RetireJS

Once it's installed, we may specify the target project to be scanned. In our example, we will scan the whole project under the `/NodeGoat/` path:

```
$ retire   --path   ~/NodeGoat/   --colors
```

Step 3 – review the retireJS results

The RetireJS scanning results show critical issues in red. There are two major known vulnerabilities with these JavaScript libraries:

Component	Severity	CVE
jquery 1.10.2	Medium	CVE-2015-9251
bootstrap 3.0.0	Medium	CVE-2018-14041

The following screenshot shows the retireJS scanning results for the NodeGoat project:

```
retire.js v2.0.1
Loading from cache: https://raw.githubusercontent.com/RetireJS/retire.js/master/repository/jsrepository.json
Loading from cache: https://raw.githubusercontent.com/RetireJS/retire.js/master/repository/npmrepository.json
/home/osboxes/NodeGoat/app/assets/vendor/jquery.min.js
 ↳ jquery 1.10.2
jquery 1.10.2 has known vulnerabilities: severity: medium; issue: 2432, summary: 3rd party CORS request may execute
, CVE: CVE-2015-9251; https://github.com/jquery/jquery/issues/2432 http://blog.jquery.com/2016/01/08/jquery-2-2-and
-1-12-released/ https://nvd.nist.gov/vuln/detail/CVE-2015-9251 http://research.insecurelabs.org/jquery/test/ severi
ty: medium; CVE: CVE-2015-9251, issue: 11974, summary: parseHTML() executes scripts in event handlers; https://bugs
.jquery.com/ticket/11974 https://nvd.nist.gov/vuln/detail/CVE-2015-9251 http://research.insecurelabs.org/jquery/tes
t/
/home/osboxes/NodeGoat/app/assets/vendor/bootstrap/bootstrap.js
 ↳ bootstrap 3.0.0
bootstrap 3.0.0 has known vulnerabilities: severity: medium; issue: 20184, summary: XSS in data-target property of
scrollspy, CVE: CVE-2018-14041; https://github.com/twbs/bootstrap/issues/20184 severity: medium; issue: 20184, summ
ary: XSS in collapse data-parent attribute, CVE: CVE-2018-14040; https://github.com/twbs/bootstrap/issues/20184 sev
erity: medium; issue: 20184, summary: XSS in data-container property of tooltip, CVE: CVE-2018-14042; https://githu
b.com/twbs/bootstrap/issues/20184
```

RetireJS scanning report

WebGoat with OWASP dependency check

In addition to RetireJS, we will also the OWASP dependency check to scan all the files of the NodeGoat project for known vulnerable libraries. Follow these steps for the OWASP dependency check scan.

Step 1 – prepare WebGoat environment

To better demonstrate the scanning results of the OWASP dependency check, we will use the WebGoat project instead of NodeGoat. The WebGoat project can be downloaded from Git. WebGoat is a purpose-built vulnerable web project used to practice security testing:

```
$ git    clone    https://github.com/WebGoat/WebGoat
```

We will also use the latest version of OWASP dependency-check, which can be downloaded here: https://bintray.com/jeremy-long/owasp/dependency-check.

Step 2 – dependency check scan

To execute the dependency-check, locate the \dependency-check\bin\ path. Execute the BAT under Windows or the SH under Linux. Refer to the following command for the WebGoat project scan:

```
$ dependency-check --project WebGoat --format XML --scan d:\tools\WebGoat
```

```
$ dependency-check --project WebGoat --format HTML --scan d:\tools\WebGoat
```

The XML report format can be useful to import into other security management tools.

It will take a while to download the NVD CVE. If you would like to do the scan without downloading the NVD CVE, you may specify the --noupdate option.

Step 3 – review the OWASP dependency-check report

After the scan, the report will be generated under the `\dependency-check\bin\` execution path. The filenames are `dependency-check-report.html` and the `dependency-check-report.xml`:

Dependency	CPE	Coordinates	Highest Severity↓	CVE Count	CPE Confidence	Evidence Count
webgoat-server-8.0.0.M21.jar: jruby-complete-1.7.21.jar: jopenssl.jar	cpe:/a:openssl:openssl:0.9.7 cpe:/a:openssl_project:openssl:0.9.7 cpe:/a:jruby:jruby:0.9.7	rubygems:jruby-openssl:0.9.7	High	100	Highest	18
webgoat-server-8.0.0.M21.jar: postgresql-42.2.2.jar	cpe:/a:postgresql:postgresql:42.2.2 cpe:/a:postgresql:postgresql_jdbc_driver:42.2.2	org.postgresql:postgresql:42.2.2 ✓	High	1	Low	45
webgoat-server-8.0.0.M21.jar: jruby-complete-1.7.21.jar (shaded: org.jruby:yecht:1.0)	cpe:/a:jruby:jruby:1.0	org.jruby:yecht:1.0	High	3	Highest	9
webgoat-server-8.0.0.M21.jar: jruby-complete-1.7.21.jar (shaded: org.jruby.extras:bytelist:1.0.11)	cpe:/a:jruby:jruby:1.0.11	org.jruby.extras:bytelist:1.0.11	High	3	Low	11
webgoat-server-8.0.0.M21.jar: jruby-complete-1.7.21.jar: readline.jar	cpe:/a:jruby:jruby:1.0	org.jruby:readline:1.0	High	3	Highest	19
webgoat-server-8.0.0.M21.jar: jruby-complete-1.7.21.jar: jruby.dll	cpe:/a:jruby:jruby:-		High	3	Low	2
webgoat-server-8.0.0.M21.jar: asciidoctor-1.5.4.jar: jruby_cache_backend.jar	cpe:/a:jruby:jruby:-		High	3	Low	8
webgoat-server-8.0.0.M21.jar: tomcat-embed-8.5.29.jar	cpe:/a:apache:tomcat:8.5.29 cpe:/a:apache_tomcat:apache_tomcat:8.5.29 cpe:/a:apache_software_foundation:tomcat:8.5.29	org.apache.tomcat.embed:tomcat-embed-core:8.5.29 ✓	High	4	Highest	21

Dependency check report

Secure communication scan with SSLScan

In this demonstration, we will inspect vulnerable security configurations with HTTPS. The tool we will be using is SSLScan. Follow these steps to perform the scan.

Step 1 – SSLScan setup

SSLSCan is a C program that can be downloaded with git clone:

```
$ git   clone   https://github.com/rbsec/sslscan
```

Once it's downloaded on Linux, use `make static` to build the SSLSCan tool:

```
$ make static
```

Step 2 – SSLScan scan

To execute sslscan, we will specify the output as XML, and also specify the target website's URL:

```
$ sslscan --no-failed --xml=nodegoat_SSLscan.xml  nodegoat.kerokuapp.com
```

`--no-failed` means only *accepted* connections will be listed in the test results. When reviewing the SSLSCan test results, we will only focus on those connections with *accepted*.

Step 3 – review the SSLScan results

Here are the SSLScan results without the options of `--no-failed`. Please focus on connections with *accepted* only. When reading the SSLScan test results, we will focus on weak HTTPS protocols and encryption algorithms such as SSL v3, TLS v1.0, TLS v1.1, and NULL. Generally, the following will be considered as vulnerable:

- SSLv2 and SSLv3
- Symmetric encryption algorithms smaller than 112 bits
- X509 certificates with RSA or DSA keys smaller than 2048 bits
- Weak hash algorithms such as MD5

This screenshot shows the sslScan results for the NodeGoat website:

SSLScan report

In addition to SSLScan, we can also use SSLTest, SSLyze, or NAMP for SSL configuration inspection.

> To read the SSLScan test results, focus on the connections with *accepted* or specify `--no-failed` to reduce unnecessary information.

Step 4 – fix the HTTPS secure configurations

The secure HTTPS configuration of a website can be very tedious and prone to mistakes. It's suggested to use the Mozilla SSL configuration generator. It will help to generate secure SSL configurations based on the web server. Refer to `https://mozilla.github.io/server-side-tls/ssl-config-generator/` for details.

NMAP security scan with BDD framework

The test results for NMAP may be difficult to understand and take time to interpret for non-security professionals. The purpose of integration with BDD and NMAP allows us to define the NMAP execution in plain English. In this example, we will use NAMP to execute some common web security tests with an **NMAP NSE (NMAP Scripting Engine)** script. Due to the execution of NMAP and the scanning results can be difficult to interpret, we will apply the Gauntlt framework to execute NMAP. Please be reminded that NAMP web security testing cannot replace a web scanner such as ZAP, due to the limitations of the security payloads and detection engine of NMAP.

NMAP For web security testing

We will be using the NMAP NSE for the following security testing: security header check, HTTP slow DOS check, SSL cipher check, XSSed history check, SQL injection check, and stored XSS check.

This table lists the NMAP security testing scenario, the NSE script we will need, and the expected results:

NMAP security testing	NMAP NSE script and scan	Expected results
Security header check	`nmap -p80 --script http-security-headers <host>`	`"X-Frame-Options: DENY"`
HTTP slow DOS check	`nmap -p80,443 --script http-slowloris-check <host>`	Should not contain `"LIKELY VULNERABLE"`
SSL ciphers check	`nmap --script=ssl-enum-ciphers <host>`	Should not contain `"SSL"`
XSSed history check	`nmap -p80 --script http-xssed.nse <host>`	Should return `"No previously reported XSS vuln"`
SQL injection check	`nmap -sV --script=http-sql-injection <host>`	Should not return `"Possible sqli for"`
Stored XSS check	`nmap -p80 --script http-stored-xss.nse <host>`	Should return `"Couldn't find any stored XSS vulnerabilities"`

NMAP NSE scripts can be downloaded here:
`https://svn.nmap.org/nmaps/scripts/<NSE script name>`. For example, the security header check NSE is at `https://svn.nmap.org/nmap/scripts/http-security-headers.nse`.

The `-oX` option can be used to generate the output in an XML-format file:

```
$ nmap -p80 --script http-security-headers nodegoat.kerokuapp.com  -oX
nodeGoat_NmapScan_HTTPheaders.xml
```

We will be using these NMAP security testing commands and expected results to integrate with the BDD framework Gauntlt in the following demonstrations.

NMAP BDD testing with Gauntlt

In this lab, we will be using NMAP with the Gauntlt BDD testing framework to test the NodeGoat website. The key structure of the Gauntlt includes scenario, When, and Then. The *scenario* is used to describe the testing case. The **When I launch a ...attack with...** is used to define the tools and command options to execute the testing. Finally, the **Then the output should is** to define the expected results. It will make the whole script and the testing results. In this demonstration, we will have the following security testing scenarios:

- **Scenario**: Verify the security header using http-security-headers
- **Scenario**: Verify the server is vulnerable to a HTTP slow DOS attack
- **Scenario**: Verify the use of insecure SSL
- **Scenario**: Was there any reported XSS history for the website
- **Scenario**: Verify any potential SQL injection into the website
- **Scenario**: Verify any potential Stored XSS

The NMAP Guantlt script will be defined as follows, with the filename
`nmap_NodeGoat_gauntlt.attack`:

```
@slow
```

Feature: nmap attacks for website. It will cover the following tesitng
security header check, HTTP Slow DOS check, SSL cipher check, XSSed History
Check, SQL Injection and the Stored XSS.

  Background:
  Given "nmap" is installed
  And the following profile:
  | name | value |
  | host | nodegoat.kerokuapp.com |

  Scenario: Verify the security header using the http-security-headers
  When I launch a "nmap" attack with:
  """
  nmap -p80 --script http-security-headers <host>
  """
  Then the output should contain "X-Frame-Options: DENY"

    Scenario: Verify if the server is vulnerable to HTTP SLOW DOS attack
    When I launch an "nmap" attack with:
    """
    nmap -p80,443 --script http-slowloris-check <host>
    """
    Then the output should not contain:
    """
    LIKELY VULNERABLE
    """

  Scenario: Verify the uses of insecure SSL
    When I launch an "nmap" attack with:
    """
    nmap --script=ssl-enum-ciphers <host>
    """
    Then the output should not contain:
    """
    SSL
    """

  Scenario: Was there any reported XSS history of the website?
    When I launch an "nmap" attack with:
    """
    nmap -p80 --script http-xssed.nse <host>
```
```

```
"""
Then the output should contain:
"""
  No previously reported XSS vuln
"""
```

Scenario: Verify any potential SQL injection of the website.
```
When I launch an "nmap" attack with:
"""
  nmap -sV --script=http-sql-injection <host>
"""
Then the output should not contain:
"""
  Possible sqli for
"""
```

Scenario: Verify any potential Stored XSS
```
When I launch an "nmap" attack with:
"""
  nmap -p80 --script http-stored-xss.nse <host>
"""
Then the output should contain:
"""
  Couldn't find any stored XSS vulnerabilities.
"""
```

To execute the script, run the following command:

```
$ gauntlt    nmap_NodeGoat_gauntlt.attack
```

The following screenshot shows one of the testing results for Gauntlt. As you can see, the testing results will be much easier to read and understand, even for non-security professionals:

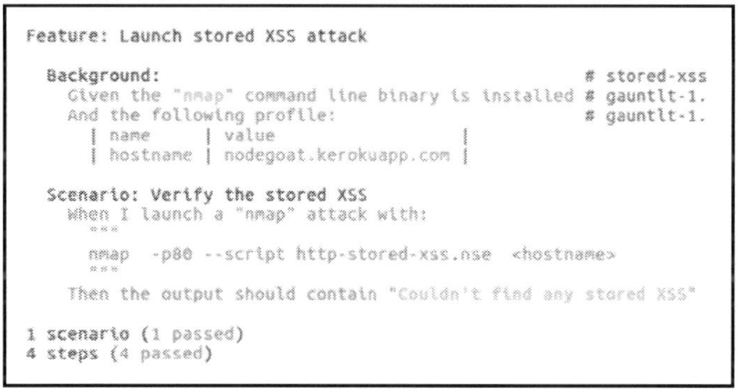

Gauntlt results

For more examples of Gauntlt, please refer to `https://github.com/gauntlt/gauntlt/tree/master/examples`.

NMAP BDD with Robot Framework

In addition to Gauntlt, we will apply Robot Framework with NMAP in this demonstration. Here are some of the key components to be used in this testing scenario:

Robot Framework key component	Use in security testing scenario
Run Process	We will use **Run Process** to execute the security testing tools. Please be aware that the command options will require double spaces in the robot Framework scripts.
${result.stdout}	Run Process will store all the output into this variable, which can be used to verify the test results.
Should Contain	We should use 'Should Contain' to verify the expected test results. In addition, Robot Framework provides other verification methods, such as 'Should Match', 'Should be Equal', 'Should End With', and 'Should be Equal As Strings'. Refer to the Robot Framework user guide 'BuiltIn' libraries for details.
Log	Log is optional. We use 'Log' to print the command execution results in the report. In our demonstration, this will be the NMAP console output results.

Step 1 – define the Robot Framework steps

If you use 'Run Process' to execute NMAP, please be aware that it will require double spaces between each parameter in the command options. Otherwise, the Robot Framework will return a file not found error even if NMAP is installed. In our example, the command options are -p80 --script http-xssed nodegoat.kerokuapp.com:

```
*** Settings ***
Library Process

*** Test Cases ***
Testing if the website was previously reported XSS
    ${result} = Run Process nmap  -p80  --script  http-xssed
nodegoat.kerokuapp.com
    Log         ${result.stdout}
    Should Contain ${result.stdout} No previously reported
```

Robot Framework has several verification keywords built in, such as 'Should Be Equal', 'Should Start With', 'Should End With' 'Should Not Match', 'Should Match Regexp', and so on. Refer to `http://robotframework.org/robotframework/latest/libraries/BuiltIn.html#Should%20Be` for more details.

Step 2 – execute and review the results

To execute the robot Framework script, use the following command:

```
$ robot      nmap_NodeGoat.robot
```

The following screenshot shows the test results for robot framework. It also generates HTML reports:

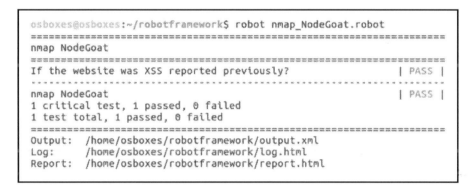

```
osboxes@osboxes:~/robotframework$ robot nmap_NodeGoat.robot
==============================================================================
nmap NodeGoat
==============================================================================
If the website was XSS reported previously?                        | PASS |
------------------------------------------------------------------------------
nmap NodeGoat                                                      | PASS |
1 critical test, 1 passed, 0 failed
1 test total, 1 passed, 0 failed
==============================================================================
Output:  /home/osboxes/robotframework/output.xml
Log:     /home/osboxes/robotframework/log.html
Report:  /home/osboxes/robotframework/report.html
```

Robot framework script execution

Here is one of the Robot framework HTML reports, `log.html`:

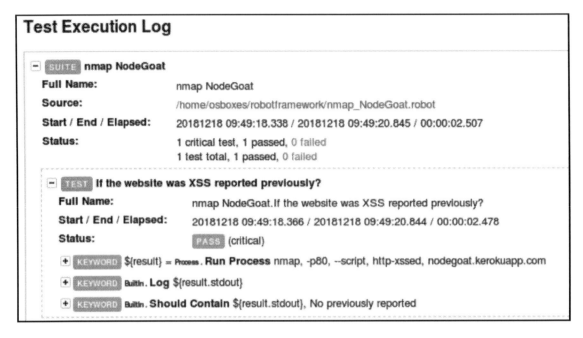

Robot framework report

Summary

In this chapter, we demonstrated infrastructure security testing against the NodeGoat website using RetireJS, OWASP dependency check, SSL communication configuration, and integration with BDD frameworks. These security testing scenarios cover the known vulnerable libraries check, secure SSL configuration check, and basic web security check.

The RetireJS and OWASP dependency check can identify the known CVE of libraries, based on a scan of their project source files. SSLScan is used to inspect any vulnerable HTTPS configurations such as SSL, short encryption keys, and weak HSA or encryption algorithms.

We also illustrated how NMAP NSE can be used to do basic web security inspections such as XSS and SQL injection. An NMAP security scan with the integration of Gauntlt and Robot Framework was also demonstrated. BDD testing techniques can help to make infrastructure security testing easier to understand and can even be maintained by a non-security team.

Questions

1. Which one best describes the purpose of RetireJS?
   1. Detect known vulnerable JavaScript libraries
   2. Scan for XSS
   3. Scan for SQL injection issues
   4. Scan for JavaScript security coding issues

2. To interpret the SSLScan results, what kind of connection should we focus on
   1. Accepted
   2. Rejected
   3. Failed
   4. Disconnected

3. Which of the following is an indicator of a weak HTTPS configuration?
   1. The use of SSL v2 or v3
   2. The use of MD5 hashing
   3. The RSA key is smaller than 1024 bits
   4. All of the above

4. What can an NMAP NSE script do for web security testing?
   1. Security header check
   2. HTTP slow DoS check
   3. SQL injection
   4. All of the above

5. What keywords are used to integrate NMAP with Robot Framework?
   1. Run process
   2. Should contain
   3. `{result.stdout}`
   4. All of the above

Further reading

- **RetireJS**: https://retirejs.github.io/retire.js/
- **Security/Server Side TLS**: https://wiki.mozilla.org/Security/Server_Side_TLS
- **NMAP NSE Index**: https://nmap.org/nsedoc/index.html
- **Robot Framework User Guide**: http://robotframework.org/robotframework/latest/libraries/BuiltIn.html#Should%20Be
- **WebMAP for NMAP reporting**: https://github.com/Rev3rseSecurity/WebMap

Managing and Presenting Test Results

14

In the previous chapters, we have introduced lots of security automation frameworks and techniques. However, how do we consolidate and present all the security findings as a whole to stakeholders? For a security team to execute and manage several security testing projects at a time can be a challenge. The security team, the project team, and the management would like to know the security status of each project. This requires us to consolidate some previously mentioned security testing tools' results into one portal or summary document. We will need to not only manage all the security testing tools' execution results, but also present a security dashboard for the overall security posture of a project. We will introduce some approaches and tools to achieve this goal.

In this chapter, we will cover the following topics:

- Managing and presenting test results
- Approach 1 – integrating the tools with RapidScan
- Approach 2 – generating a professional pentest report with Serpico
- Approach 3 – security findings management with DefectDojo

Managing and presenting test results

We have learned several security testing techniques and automation frameworks. After all the security testing is done, we will need to consolidate the security testing findings to present into a dashboard or a document to share with stakeholders. In addition to Robot Framework, which we have demonstrated, there are also other tools that can help us to do the reporting consolidation.

The screenshot shows the integration of security findings from different testing tools:

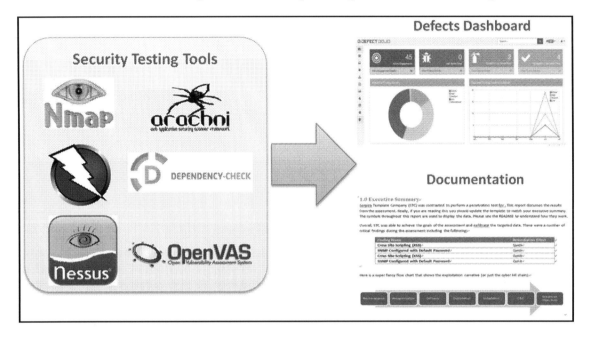

Security Testing Reporting Framework

We will introduce three typical tools to achieve consolidation of security findings:

Tools	RapidScan	OWASP DefectDojo	Serpico
Characteristics	It's a Python script that will execute several security testing tools and present the results.	It can import several open source and commercial security testing tools' reports, and present security issues in one dashboard. It can also generate a testing report document based on selected information. • Multiple team co-work • Manage several projects • Defect management dashboard	It provides a list of security findings templates (security issues and mitigation suggestions). You may apply the security findings to generate a professional document.
Generate a document	No, output to console only	Yes, PDF or ASCII	Yes, DOC
Execution	Python script: `$ python rapidscan.py`	Web service: `http://localhost:8000`	Web service: `https://localhost:8443/`
Import testing results from tools	No	Yes	No

Manage multiple projects	No	Yes	Yes
License	GNU General Public License v2.0	BSD 3-Clause	BSD 3-Clause

In addition to OWASP Defect Dojo, the following penetration testing reporting tools may also be considered. These reporting tools allow penetration testers to import the security testing output (XML) from various security testing tools:

- FaradaySEC
- Jackhammer
- Dradis Framework
- ArcherySec
- Dradis Framework

Approach 1 – integrate the tools with RapidScan

RapidScan can execute several security testing tools and output key security findings.

Step 1 – get the RapidScan Python script

To get the RapidScan script, follow these commands:

```
$ wget -O rapidscan.py
https://raw.githubusercontent.com/skavngr/rapidscan/master/rapidscan.py &&
chmod +x rapidscan.py
$ python rapidscan.py  nodegoat.herokuapp.com
```

The script will not install related security tools, but it will show a warning message for any missing security tools. It's recommended to run the RapidScan script under Kali Linux to reduce the installation of the security testing tools. The table lists the security testing tools that will be executed by the RapidScan script:

Tools	Security Testing Scenario
wapiti	It checks for SQLi, RCE, XSS, and Other Vulnerabilities
whatweb	It's used to check for X-XSS Protection security Header
nmap	In RapidScan, it's used to check listening ports, and also SSL vulnerabilities.
golismero	It's a web security scanner that can check whether the domain is spoofed, brute force attack on the target domain, and perform SSL vulnerabilities scans
host	It's used to check the existence of an IPV6 address in the RadpiScan
wget	It's used to check administrator web interfaces such as /wp-admin
uniscan	Uniscan can perform attacks such as Remote File Include, Local File Include, and Remote Command Execution. It can also do brute force for filenames and directories
wafw00f	It checks for the existence of an application firewall
dirb	Brute forces the directory traverse
davtest	Checks whether WEBDAV is enabled on the Home directory
theharvester	It uses Google to search if any email address related to the target domain
xsser	It scans for **XSS (cross-site scripting)** security issues
dnsrecon	It can check all NS Records for Zone Transfers
fierce	Fierce is a DNS reconnaissance tool used to scan for any zone transfers
dnswalk	DNSWalk is also used to check any zone transfer
whois	It's used to check the administrator contact information of the registered domain
sslyze	It checks for SSL vulnerabilities
lbd	It checks for DNS/HTTP Load Balancers
dnsenum	It checks for DNS zone transfer
dmitry	It searches for email information from the domain
davtest	It scans for enabled WebDAV enabled servers by uploading test executable files
nikto	nikto is used to scan for several web security issues such as XSS headers, subdomain traversal, internal IP disclosure, SSL vulnerabilities, sensitive files, injectable paths, and so on
dnsmap	It can brute force scan for subdomains of the target website

To execute the RapidScan, it's suggested to run it directly in Kali Linux. It will save lots of time to do the security tools installation. For detailed information on how to use each tool executed by RapidScan, refer to the Kali Tool list: https://tools.kali.org/tools-listing.

This screenshot shows the use of the RapidScan:

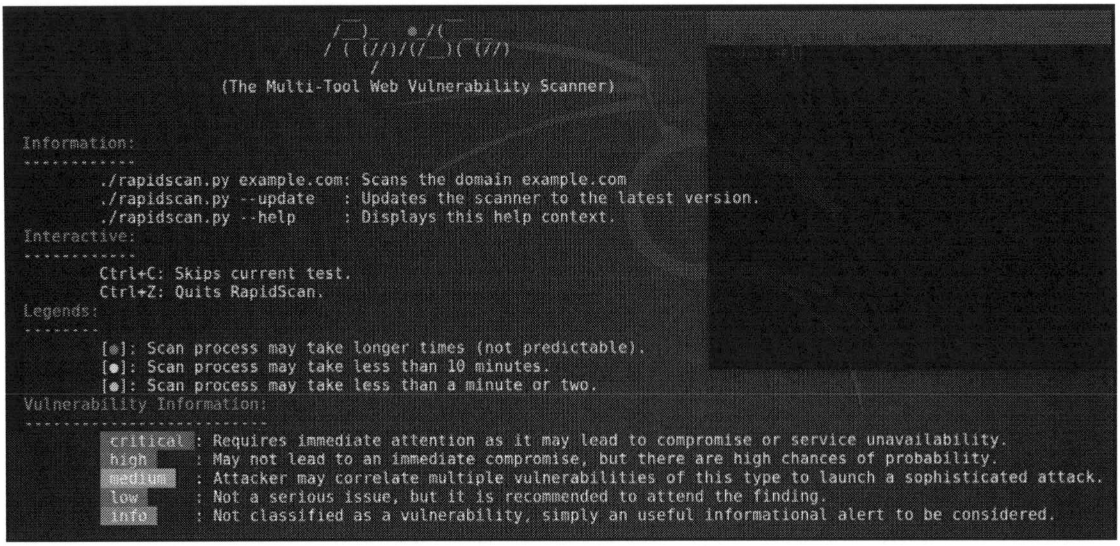

RapidScan usage

Step 2 – review scanning results

The RapidScan detects the following major security vulnerabilities:

- Nmap [STUXNET] Critical Vulnerable to STUXNET
- Nmap: Checks for Remote Desktop SErvice over TCP : High RDP Server Detected over TCP
- Uniscan detected possible XSS, SQLi, BSQLi
- Nmap [FTP] FTP Service Detected

For detailed information of report, please also refer to RS-Debug-ScanLog and RS-Vulnerability-Report.

This screenshot shows parts of the NodeGoat scanning results of the RapidScan:

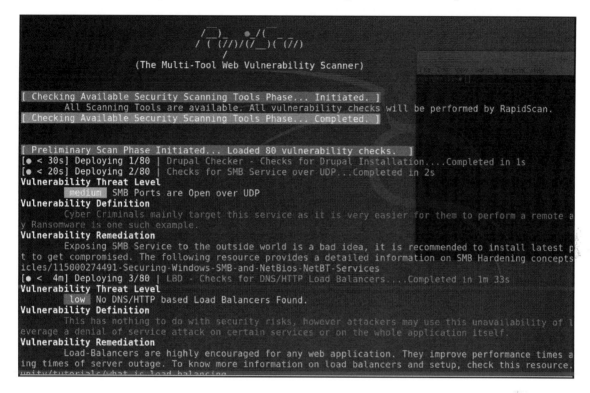

RapidScan Scan Results

Approach 2 – generate a professional pentest report with Serpico

A summary of the security testing documentation will help you to communicate with stakeholders. The report should not only list the security findings but also how they were identified, the testing scope, the methodology, and also mitigation suggestions. It's a common practice for an independent security testing firm to produce such documentation. The PCI DSS Penetration Test Guidance suggests a Penetration Test Report Outline as follows:

- Executive summary
- Statement of Scope

- Statement of methodology
- Segmentation test results
- Findings
- Tools used

Serpico is a penetration testing report generator, which can help to produce such a document. Although Serpico doesn't import the security testing results from tools, it allows users to select security findings/mitigation's based on templates. Follow the steps in the next sectionto generate your own penetration testing document.

Step 1 – installation of Serpico

Depending on the platform, download one of the installation packages here:

```
https://github.com/SerpicoProject/Serpico/releases
```

For example, we can download `serpico_1.3.0_x86.msi` for installation on Windows. Once the installation is done, Serpico can be launched with the `start_serpico.bat` script:

```
$ cd Serpico
$ start_serpico.bat
```

Then, use a browser to visit `https://localhost:8443/`.

By the time of the writing, you may ecnouter report generation error after adding images in the findings. When it occurs, try to comment out the following lines in `server.rb` to workaround the issue:

```
#elsif png?(img_data)
#width = IO.read(image.filename_location)[0x10..0x18].unpack('NN')[0]
#height =
IO.read(image.filename_location)[0x10..0x18].unpack('NN')[1]
```

Step 2 – create a Report based on Templates

To create a report, click **New Report** from the menu at the top. There are some report templates you may select, such as assessment type, and also report types such as DREAD, CVSS, and NIST 800. The key differences between these report types are the risk scoring categories.

For example, NIST 800-30 defines risk rating as shown in the following table:

		Impact of threat				
		Informational	Low	Moderate	High	Critical
Threat likelihood	High	Informational	Low	Moderate	High	Critical
	Moderate	Informational	Low	Moderate	Moderate	High
	Low	Informational	Low	Low	Moderate	Moderate

This screenshot shows **Create Report** in Serpico:

Create Report (or Import)

Title

Language   English ▾

Full Company Name

Short Company Name

Assessment Type   Network Internal ▾

Report Type   Default Template - Generic Ris ▾

- Default Template - Generic Risk Scoring
- Default Template - DREAD Scoring
- Default CVSS Report
- Default CVSSv3 Report
- Default NIST800 Report
- Default Finding

Save   Cancel

Serpico Report

Step 3 – Add Finding from Templates

After creating a report with basic project information, it's suggested to **Add Finding From Templates** instead of add every finding from scratch. The finding templates include some common attacks and mitigation information. We may edit the security findings based on these templates and project testing results.

This screenshot shows **Add Finding from Templates**:

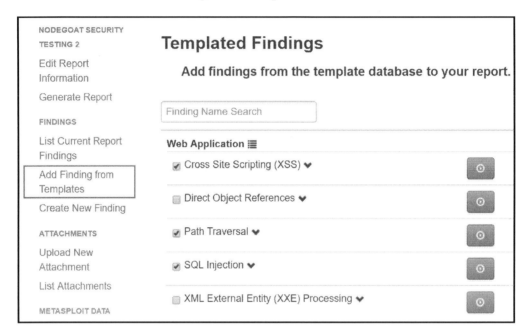

Serpico Report Templates

Step 4 – generate a report

To generate a report, click **Generate Report** on the left menu. One Word document will be automatically generated based on your selected information and security findings.

This screenshot shows a sample of a generated report in Word format:

1.0 Executive Summary

Serpico Template Company (STC) was contracted to perform a penetration test for . This report discusses the results from the assessment. Really, if you are reading this you should update the template to match your executive summary. The symbols throughout this report are used to display the data. Please see the README to understand how they work.

Overall, STC was able to achieve the goals of the assessment and exfiltrate the targeted data. There were a number of critical findings during the assessment including the following:

Finding Name	Remediation Effort
Cross Site Scripting (XSS)	Quick
SNMP Configured with Default Password	Quick
Cross Site Scripting (XSS)	Quick
SNMP Configured with Default Password	Quick

Here is a super fancy flow chart that shows the exploitation narrative (or just the cyber kill chain):

2.0 Findings

2.1 Findings Table

The following findings were made during the assessment.

Finding Name	Remediation Effort
Critical Risk Findings	
Cross Site Scripting (XSS)	Quick
SNMP Configured with Default Password	Quick
Cross Site Scripting (XSS)	Quick
SNMP Configured with Default Password	Quick
High Risk Findings	
Weak SA Password on MSSQL Server	Quick
Weak SA Password on MSSQL Server	Quick
Moderate Risk Findings	
Internal IP Address Disclosure	Quick
Internal IP Address Disclosure	Quick
Low Risk Findings	
Informational Findings	
Hard Coded Passwords in Use	Quick
Excessive Ingress Rule Set	Quick
Hard Coded Passwords in Use	Quick
Excessive Ingress Rule Set	Quick

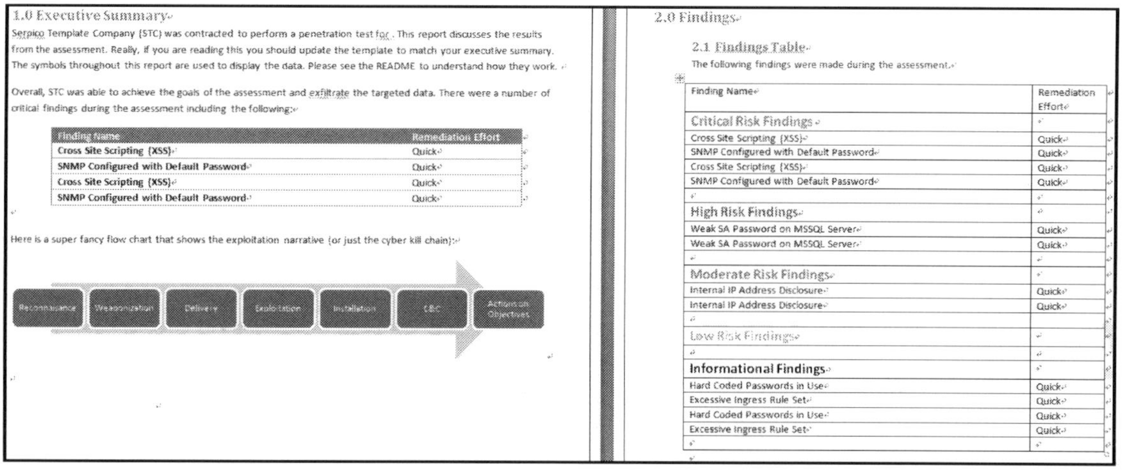

Serpico Report Sample

Approach 3 – security findings management DefectDojo

In this approach, we use several security testing tools to do security testing with XML outputs. These XML outputs will be imported into a defect management service, OWASP DefectDojo in our demonstration. The security defect management web service will help to consolidate all the testing results in one security dashboard, or even generate a summary report. Follow the steps to learn how to apply OWASP DefectDojo to manage your security findings.

Step 1 – setup the OWASP DefectDojo

To set up the OWASP DefectDojo, running the Docker image is suggested. Follow these commands to run OWASP DefectDojo. It will run a web service on port `8000`:

```
$ docker run -it -p 8000:8000 appsecpipeline/django-defectdojo bash -c
"export LOAD_SAMPLE_DATA=True && bash /opt/django-DefectDojo/docker/docker-
startup.bash"
```

Once the OWASP defectDojo docker is running, use your browser to navigate to `http://localhost:8000` with the default credentials (user: `admin`, password: `admin`).

In addition, OWASP DefectDojo also provides an online demo. Refer to `https://defectdojo.herokuapp.com` with the default credentials listed here:

Username	Password
`admin`	`defectdojo@demo#appsec`
`product_manager`	`defectdojo@demo#product`

Step 2 – run security tools to output XMLs

Generally, most security testing tools can output testing results in XML or JSON format. In our demonstration, we generate most of the results in XML files and import them into OWASP DefectDojo.

This table shows some common security testing tools for how to execute the security testing with XML output:

Tools	Security testing, output format and command options

OWASP ZAP	Web Security testing with XML output format:
	`$ zap-cli quick-scan -s xss,sqli --spider -r http://nodegoat.herokuapp.com/`
	`$ zap-cli report -o ZAP_Report.xml    -f    xml`

Dependency Check	Scan for known vulnerabilities with XML output format: `$ dependency-check.bat    --format    XML    --project NodeGoat -s d:\NodeGoat`

NMAP	Network security scanning with XML output format:
	`$ nmap    -sV    -sC    nodegoat.herokuapp.com    -oX /tmp/webmap/NodeGoat_NMAP.xml`
	`$ nmap -p80 --script http-stored-xss.nse nodegoat.herokuapp.com`
	`$ nmap -p80,443 --script http-slowloris --max-parallelism 500 -Pn    nodegoat.herokuapp.com`
	`$ nmap    -p21, 23,80, 137,138, 443, 445, 1433, 3306, 1521, 3389    --open -Pn n    odegoat.herokuapp.com`

Retire	Scan for known vulnerabilities of JavaScript libraries: `$ retire --path \nodegoat    --outputformat    json    --colors`

Step 3 – import ZAP findings

Once we have done the web security testing by using OWASP ZAP, the `ZAP_Report.xml` file can be imported into OWASP DefectDojo. Before we can import the security findings XML file, we need to create a product and engagement:

- **Add Product**: OWASP DefectDojo can manage several products (projects). For example, NodeGoat is our product in this case.
- **Add New Engagement**: Engagement can be every planned security testing cycle. There may be several engagements due to different kinds of security testing tools or several periods of testing.

We will use **Add New Engagement** | **Import Scan results** to import the ZAP XML testing results `ZAP_Report.xml`:

DefectDojo with ZAP Import

Once the XML import is done, you may review the security findings in the web console. If there are several projects or engagements for security testing, you will find such a dashboard helpful for the communication and presentation of the security status:

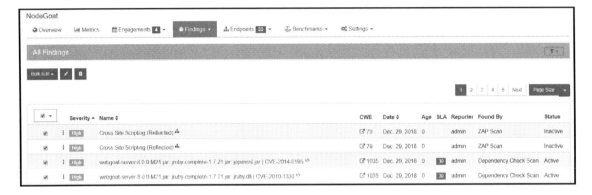

Findings in DefectDojo

In addition, OWASP defectDojo also includes **Report Builder** to generate a PDF document.

Summary

A well-documented report can not only help you to communicate with stakeholders, but also demonstrate the value of security testing. A professional penetration testing report should include an agenda such as executive summary, statement of scope, statement of methodology, test results, findings, mitigations, and tools used.

In this chapter, we have introduced three approaches to managing the testing results. First, we can use the script to integrate all the testing results. We demonstrated the uses of a Python script, RapidScan, which executes several security testing tools and presents the security findings in a console with highlighted colors. Secondly, we also introduced the document generator Serpico, which can help to generate professional penetration testing documentation, which includes the summary, security findings, risk ratings, and mitigations. Finally, we applied a reporting management service, which can import all the XML testing results and present the findings in one dashboard. We have illustrated this by using OWASP DefectDojo.

Questions

1. What should be included in a penetration testing report?
    1. Executive summary
    2. Statement of methodology
    3. Findings
    4. All of above

2. How does NIST 800-30 categorize risk rating?
    1. Impact of Threat vs Threat Likelihood
    2. Severity vs Impact
    3. Impact vs Mitigation efforts
    4. Severity vs Asset Value

3. What is the common report format that can be imported into the reporting service?
    1. HTML
    2. XML
    3. CSV
    4. DOC

4. Which one of these is not used for web security testing?
    1. `nmap`
    2. `uniscan`
    3. `dirb`
    4. `IDA`

5. Which one is not used for network scanning?
    1. `nmap`
    2. `xsser`
    3. `dnsenum`
    4. `dnsmap`

Further reading

- **Web security scanner Arachni**: https://github.com/Arachni/arachni
- **Arachni**: https://github.com/Arachni/arachni/wiki/Installation
- **Archerysec**: https://github.com/archerysec/archerysec
- **DefectDojo Demo Site**: https://defectdojo.herokuapp.com (admin / defectdojo@demo#appsec)
- **Archerysec Demo Site**: https://archerysec-test.herokuapp.com/webscanners (**Username**: archerysec, **Password**: archerysec@archerysec)
- **Serpico Report templates**: https://github.com/SerpicoProject/Serpico/tree/master/templates
- **PCI Penetration Testing Guidance**: https://www.pcisecuritystandards.org/documents/Penetration_Testing_Guidance_March_2015.pdf
- **OWASP DefectDojo**: https://github.com/DefectDojo/django-DefectDojo

15

Summary of Automation
Security Testing Tips

This chapter summarizes key security automation techniques and tips of all previously discussed chapters. This chapter can be used as a quick reference guide or as an overall review for the following security automation topics:

- Automation testing framework
- Secure code review
- API security testing
- Web security testing
- Android security testing
- Infrastructure security
- BDD security testing by Robot Framework

Automation testing framework

We have introduced the automation framework for the functional web, mobile, and Windows UI testing. We also introduced the adoption of BDD framework with security testing. In terms of the layers of automation approaches, white-box testing, API testing, and Web UI automation are also demonstrated. We will list key questions and answers regarding tips concerning security automation techniques.

What are the automation frameworks for UI functional testing?

The following table lists common automation frameworks for Web UI functional testing:

Automation frameworks	Macaca	AutoIT	Selenium	Appium	Sikuli
Testing target	Mobile (iOS and Android) Web UI	Windows applications	Web UI	Mobile (iOS/Android)	Visual image
Programming languages	Java, Python, NodeJS	BASIC-like script	Java, Python, C#, Ruby	Java, Python	Image and BASIC-like script
Record and replay	UI recorder	AutoIT recorder	Selenium IDE	Desktop inspector	Yes

BDD (behavior-driven development) testing framework?

The following table lists the key usages and scenarios of BDD testing frameworks:

BDD framework	Usage and scenarios
Robot Framework	It's a common keyword driven testing acceptance automation framework. The Robot Framework is programming language independent though the Robot Framework itself was built by Python. `http://robotframework.org`
Behave	It's a Python BDD framework `https://github.com/behave/behave`
JGiven	It's a Java BDD framework `http://jgiven.org/`
Gauntlt	It's a purpose-built for security BDD framework in Ruby `http://gauntlt.org/`

What are common automation frameworks that apply to security testing?

The following table lists the common automation testing tools and applied scenarios:

Automation approaches	Mapping to security testing scenarios	Example of automation tools/framework
White Box	• Secure code inspection • Secure configuration inspection	• Secure code analysis such as **VCG** (**Visual code Grepper**)
API testing	• Web/RESTful API security testing • Parameterized (data-driven) with Fuzz testing	• Robot Framework requests library • JMeter • FuzzDB • OWASP ZAP
Web UI automation	• Login with different users or wrong accounts. • Logout users for session management testing. • Create a new user account. • Brute force user account login.	• Robot Framework • Selenium • OWASP ZAP

Secure code review

For the source code security review, we listed common source code patterns of critical security issues and also risky APIs. Based on these security source patterns, we also introduced some open source tools to search these security issues.

What are common secure code review patterns and risky APIs?

The following table lists common keywords and patterns for secure code review:

Programming language	Risky API or the insecure code patterns		False positive
General	Weak encryption	`Blowfish	DES	3DES	RC4	MD5	SHA1	XOR	ARC4	IDEA	ECB	CBC	TLS 1.0	SSL 2.0	Base64	RIPEMD`	Low
	Insecure protocol	`SSL	HTTP	FTP	Telnet`	Low
	Hard-coded info.	`Password	IP address	Email	Special Hotkey	URL	Mobile Number	Name`	High

C/C++	Command injection	`execl|execlp|execle|system|popen|WinExec|ShellExecute| execv|execvp|`	Med
	Buffer overflow	`fscanf|sscanf|vsscanf|vfscanf | scanf|vscanf|wscanf| sprintf|vsprintf|swprintf|vswprintf| getchar| read|_gettc | fgetc|getc| memcpy|CopyMemory|bcopy lstrcpy|wcscpy| lstrcpyn|wcsncpy | _tcscpy|_mbscpy`	Low
Java	Injection	`Runtime | ProcessBuilder | CommandLine | zookeeper.Shell | System.out.printf | createStatement`	Low
	Path traversal	`getAbsolutePath`	Low
	Deserialization	`XMLDecoder | xstream | readObject | readResolve | InvocationHandle`	Med
	Weak random	`Java.util.Random`	Low
	XXE	`DocumentBuilder | XMLInputFactory | SAXReader | SAXParser | SAXBuilder | XMLReader | DocumentHelper | XMLInputFactory | XMLStreamReader`	Med
	ZIP of Death	`ZipFile | ZipInputStream`	Med
Python	Injection	`execfile | input | commands | subprocess`	Med
	Risky API	`pickle.load | eval`	Med
PHP	Injection	`shell_exec | system | exec | popen | passthru | proc_open | pcntl_exec | eval | assert | preg_replace | create_function`	Low
JavaScript	Risky API	`eval | execScript | sessionStorage | localStorage`	Low

Suggestions with Grep-like search tool for source code or configurations search?

The following table lists the suggested tools for source code search:

Search tools	Key characteristics
Code review audit script scanner	It's one shell script that includes all common secure code issue patterns. No other dependency is required to run the script. `https://github.com/floyd-fuh/crass/blob/master/grep-it.sh`
Grep rough audit	It's also a shell script that will read the signatures for a potential security issue in the source code. `https://github.com/wireghoul/graudit/`
GrepBugs	It scans security issues based on defined regular expression patterns. `https://grepbugs.com/browse`

VisualCodeGrepper	It's a Windows scanner tool with defined regular expression security patterns. `https://github.com/nccgroup/VCG`
Flawfinder	It's a simple C/C++ security source code scanner. `http://www.dwheeler.com/flawfinder/`
ripgrep recursively searches	It's a powerful regular expression searcher. `https://github.com/BurntSushi/ripgrep`

API security testing

For API testing, we applied ZAP and JMeter with the FuzzDB security payloads. The ZAP itself can be used to send malicious APIs and also analyze the HTTP responses for the security issues. On the other hand, JMeter is mainly used to send the HTTP requests with FuzzDB security payloads by using **CSV Config Element**. Furthermore, there are also other approaches to do the fuzzing testing, such as Selenium with **data-driven testing** (DDT) module, Robot Framework with DDT, as well as Od1n and Wfuzz.

What are API security testing approaches?

The following table lists the API security testing tools and approaches:

Level	Recommended toolkits	Pros and cons
Basic	ZAP	ZAP can provide a general web security baseline scan. However, ZAP can't do specific REST or SOAP API security testing without proper guidance. For example, the HTTP POST request testing can't be done here, and that's why we introduce JMeter for the next level.

Intermediate	ZAP + JMeter	The rationale we introduce JMeter is to send specific REST or SOAP APIs and message body through ZAP. In this approach, the ZAP will be running in proxy mode to monitor and detect the request/response for security issues.
Advanced	ZAP + JMeter + Fuzz data	We will use JMeter with parameterized testing (data driven testing). The Fuzz data is a dictionary list of specific security issues, such as XSS, SQL injection, or common vulnerable password. Although ZAP itself also includes the Fuzz testing that can replace the specified parameters with Fuzz data, ZAP Fuzz testing can only be done by GUI mode at this moment. By using the ZAP and JMeter, we can execute the automation in command console mode for the integration with other CI frameworks.
Advanced	ZAP + OpenAPI	In this case, the ZAP will import the API definition files, and do the initial security assessment based on the API lists.

What are the suggested resources for FuzzDB security payloads?

The following table lists of sources of FuzzDB for security testing payloads:

Fuzz database	Description
FuzzDB	FuzzDB compressive application security testing dictionary for attack patterns (injection, XSS, directory traversals), Discovery (admin directories or sensitive files), response analysis (regular expression patterns), web backdoors samples and `user/pwd` list. `https://github.com/fuzzdb-project/fuzzdb`
Naughty Strings	The Naughty Strings provides a very long list of strings. There are two formats provided, `blns.txt` and `blns.json`. `https://github.com/minimaxir/big-list-of-naughty-strings`
Seclists	This is similar to FuzzDB which provides various kinds of Fuzz data, such as command injections, JSON, LDAP, User agents, XSS, char, numeric, Unicode data and so on. `https://github.com/danielmiessler/SecLists`
Radamsa	Unlike previous FuzzDB providing a list of word dictionary, it's a tool that can dynamically generate format-specific based on a given sample. `https://github.com/vah13/radamsa`

What testing tools are suggested for web fuzz testing?

The following table lists the key characteristics of various technical approaches to implement fuzz testing:

	OWASP ZAP	JMeter	Selenium DDT	Robot framework DDT	0d1n	Wfuzz
Dependency	No	OWASP ZAP	OWASP ZAP	CSVLibrary	OWASP ZAP	No
Coding	No	No	Yes but Selenium IDE can help to generate the script.	No	No	No
Fuzz data handing	ZAP UI mode only	CSV Config in Jmeter	DDT library in Python	CSV library For Loop	∧ in the command line	FUZZ or FUZ2Z keyword

Testing report	Refer to OWASP ZAP	Refer to OWASP ZAP	Refer to OWASP ZAP	Refer to OWASP ZAP	Refer to OWASP ZAP	Output to the console or file
Fuzz multiple parameters	Yes	Yes	Yes	Yes	Yes, but other value may be filled as empty.	Yes `FUZZ, FUZ2Z, FUZ3Z...`
Integration interface	No	RESTful APIs JMeter script	Selenium scripts	Robot Framework scripts	Command line (CLI)	CLI
Testing framework popularity	The API and CLI don't support fuzz testing at this moment.	High JMeter is common in REST API and performance testing.	High Common Web UI framework.	High Common acceptance testing framework.	Low 0d1n is specifically built for fuzz testing in CLI.	MED
Launch browser during the testing	No	No	Yes	Yes	No	No

Please also refer to the following diagram to understand the role of the tools used in web security testing:

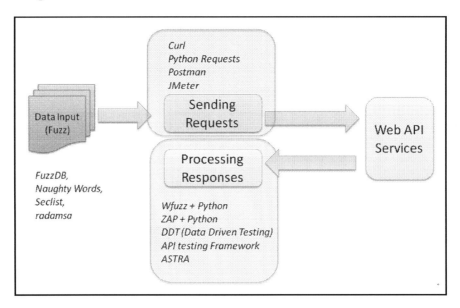

API Fuzz testing framework

Web security testing

To automate the web security testing, we have learned to operate the ZAP by using RESTful API and also the ZAP-CLI.

How can JMeter be used for the web security testing?

The following diagram shows that the JMeter is used to send the HTTP request with the security payloads from FuzzDB. The ZAP is running as the web proxy to assess the HTTP requests/responses to identify potential security issues:

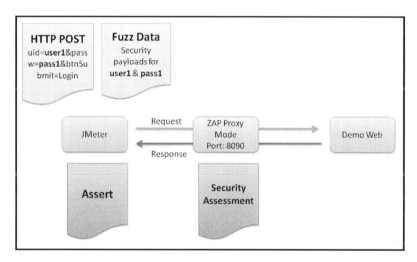

Security testing with JMeter and ZAP

Examples of OWASP ZAP by ZAP-CLI usages

The following command will trigger the web Spider scan, xss, and SQL injection security scan toward the nodeGoat website:

```
$ zap-cli quick-scan -s xss,sqli --spider -r http://nodegoat.herokuapp.com/
```

The following command will generate a report in HTML format:

```
$ zap-cli report -o ZAP_Report.html -f html
```

Examples of OWASP ZAP automation by RESTful API

The following table lists the ZAP operations:

ZAP operations	Restful API usage example
Spider scan of hackazon website	`CURL http://localhost:8090/JSON/spider/action/scan /?zapapiformat=JSON&formMethod=GET&url =http://hackazon.webscantest.com`
Active scan of the hackazon site	`CURL http://localhost:8090/JSON/ascan/action/scan/?zapapiformat =JSON&formMethod=GET&url= http://hackazon.webscantest.com&recurse=&inScopeOnly =&scanPolicyName=&method=&postData=&contextId=`
Generate testing report in HTML	`CURL http://127.0.0.1:8090/OTHER/core/other/htmlreport/?formMethod=GET" > ZAP_Report.HTML`
Shutdown the ZAP	`CURL http://localhost:8090/JSON/core/action/`**`shutdown`**`/ ?zapapiformat=JSON&formMethod=GET`

Android security testing

Then Android application security testing techniques include the source code scan, privacy information inspection, reverse engineering of an APK, and the adoption of automated security testing frameworks, such as QARK and MobSF.

Suggested Android security testing tools and approach

The following table lists the Android security scanning and tools:

Scanning approach	Automated tools	Description
Secure code scanning	Fireline	Static Java source code scanning. It's a light-weight secure code scanning tools, but it may require the Java source and the reverse of APK.

Privacy and sensitive information scan	Androwarn	It's focused on privacy and sensitive information scanning of any given APK. Static analysis of the application's Dalvik bytecode, represented as Smali for PII and sensitive information leakage or exfiltration such as telephony identifiers, geolocation information leakage, audio/video flow interception, and so on.
Light-weight all in one APK security scanning	**QARK (Quick Android Review Kit)**	It's a Python program that can do automatically security scanning of any given APK.
All in one security scanning	**Mobile Security Framework (MobSF)**	The MobSF is similar to QARK. In addition, MobSF supports Android, Windows, and iOS applications. It not only does the static security analysis, but also does dynamic runtime behavior analysis.

Common Android security risky APIs

The following table lists down the high risk APIs:

Security inspection focuses	Related high-risk APIs and keywords
SQL injection	`rawQuery	execSQL	database	.sqlite	SQLiteDatabase`
Insecure SSL handling	`ALLOW_ALL_HOST_VERIFIER	NullHostnameVerifier SSLCertificateSocketFactory	SSLSocketFactory setDefaultHostnameVerifier WebViewClient.onReceivedSslError`
Command injection	`getRuntime	ClassLoader`
WebView for XSS	`Android.webkit	setJavaScriptEnabled	addJavascriptInterface	setWebContentsDebuggingEnabled(true) loadData	postURL`
Insecure files I/O access	`MODE_WORLD_READABLE	MODE_WORLD_WRITTABLE OpenFileOutput	openORCreateDatabase file://	getSharedPreferences	getExternal`
Insecure communication	`.netURL	openSteam	netJarURL	HttpURL	HttpRqeuest	HttpsURL`

Infrastructure security

The scope of infrastructure security testing covers the known vulnerable components inspection, secure configurations, and secure communication protocols. In addition to the uses of tools, the industry organization best practices, including CIS benchmarks, STIG, and OpenSCAP are also introduced.

What's the scope of infrastructure security testing?

The following describes the scope of infrastructure security testing:

Infrastructure/platform security	Description	Open source tools and resources
Known vulnerable components	The known vulnerable (CVE) component is one of OWASP top 10 threats. If one component is exploited, the application can be vulnerable to remote injection or data leakage security risks.	• OpenVAS • Nmap • OWASP Dependency Check • RetireJS
Secure configuration	The secure configuration is to ensure the OS, Web, virtualization, and databases are configured securely, such as password complexity, removal of default settings, or disable unnecessary services.	• OpenSCAP • CIS benchmarks • STIG
Insecure network communication	The followings secure communication protocols version should be used: • SFTP instead of FTP • TLS 1.2 instead of HTTP, SSL, and TLS 1.1 • SNMP V3 instead of v1/v2 • SSH v2 instead of SSH v1 or Telnet	• Nmap • SSLyze

Typical use of Nmap for security testing

The following table shows typical uses of Nmap for security testing:

Common network security assessments scenarios	NMap command
Fast scan for listening ports	`nmap -F --open -Pn`
Scan for any missing http security headers such as XSS-Protection	`nmap -p80 --script http-security-headers -Pn`
DOS attack with HTTPS Slowloris	`nmap -p80,443 --script http-slowloris --max-parallelism 500 -Pn`
Scanning for all TCP listening ports	`nmap -p1-65535 --open -Pn`
Scanning for all UDP listening ports	`nmap -p1-65535 -sU --open -Pn`
Scanning for common ports	`Nmap -p21, 23,80, 137,138, 443, 445, 1433, 3306, 1521, 3389 --open -Pn`

The following table shows Nmap security testing with its expected results:

Nmap security tesitng	Nmap NSE script and scan	Expected results
Security header check	`nmap -p80 --script http-security-headers <host>`	**X-Frame-Options: DENY**
HTTP SLOW DOS check	`nmap -p80,443 --script http-slowloris-check <host>`	Should not contain **LIKELY VULNERABLE**
SSL ciphers check	`nmap --script=ssl-enum-ciphers <host>`	Should not contain **SSL**
XSSed history check	`nmap -p80 --script http-xssed.nse <host>`	Should return **No previously reported XSS vuln**
SQL injection	`nmap -sV --script=http-sql-injection <host>`	Should not return **Possible sqli for**
Stored XSS	`nmap -p80 --script http-stored-xss.nse <host>`	Should return **Couldn't find any stored XSS vulnerabilities**

BDD security testing by Robot Framework

The adoption of BDD security testing defines the testing steps into *Given, When, Then* English language structure. We demonstrated the uses of Robot Framework and the Gauntlt BDD framework.

How to do web security scan with ZAP and Robot Framework?

The following script will do a OWASP ZAP **Spider Scan** on demo.testfire.net to explore all the potential Web URLs and resources:

```
*** Settings ***
 Suite Teardown Delete All Sessions
 Library Collections
 Library String
 Library RequestsLibrary
 Library OperatingSystem

*** Variables ***
 ${url}                    http://demo.testfire.net
 ${SpiderScan}
http://localhost:8090/JSON/spider/action/scan/?zapapiformat=JSON&formMethod
=GET&url=${url}&maxChildren=&recurse=&contextName=&subtreeOnly=

*** Test Cases ***
 ZAP Spider Scan
 [Tags] get skip
 Create Session    ZAP      ${SpiderScan}
 ${resp}=    Get Request    ZAP    /
 Should Be Equal As Strings    ${resp.status_code}    200
```

How to achieve DDT testing in Robot Framework?

The following is a Robot Framework sample script to do DDT testing that reads the data from `sqli.csv` and tests against `userName` and `password` parameters of the NodeGoat website. Please be reminded that the Robot Framework itself can't do sophisticated security analysis based on the HTTP response. Therefore, it's suggested to run OWASP ZAP as a proxy between the Robot Framework and the target testing website. The sample script is as follows:

```
*** Settings ***
Library Collections
Library CSVLibrary
Library SeleniumLibrary
Library OperatingSystem
Library String
Library Collections

*** Test Cases ***
SignIn_DDT
    Open Browser http://nodegoat.herokuapp.com/login
    @{data}= read csv file to list sqli.csv
    Log ${data}
    :FOR ${x} IN @{data}
    \ Log ${x}
    \ Input Text id=userName ${x[${0}]}
    \ Input Text id=password ${x[${1}]}
    \ Click Button xpath=//button[@type='submit']
    \ Log ${x[${0}]}
    \ Log ${x[${1}]}
    Close Browser
```

The preceding Robot Framework script is based on the CSV `sqli.csv` as follows:

```
username,password
a,pass1
b,pass2
c,''
d,' or 1=1
```

How to do network scan with Nmap and Robot Framework?

The following sample Robot Framework script will execute the Nmap testing with expected results verification:

```
*** Settings ***
Library Process

*** Test Cases ***
Testing if the website was previously reported XSS
    ${result} = Run Process nmap  -p80  --script  http-xssed
nodegoat.kerokuapp.com
    Log          ${result.stdout}
    Should Contain ${result.stdout} No previously reported
```

How to do an SQLmap scan with Robot Framework?

The following sample Robot Framework script will execute the SQLmap (SQL injection) testing with expected results verification:

```
*** Settings ***
Library SSHLibrary
*** Variables ***
${HOST_URL} http://demo.testfire.net

*** Test Cases ***
SQL Injection Testing
[Documentation] Use SQLmap to do the SQL injection testing on target host
${output}= Execute Command python sqlmap.py -u ${HOST_URL} -- batch --
banner
Should Not Contain ${output} vulnerable
```

How to do BDD security testing with Nmap and Gauntlt?

The following is a Gauntlt, BDD testing framework sample script to do Nmap security testing:

```
@slow

Feature: nmap attacks for website. It will cover the following tesitng
security header check, HTTP Slow DOS check, SSL cipher check, XSSed History
Check, SQL Injection and the Stored XSS.

    Background:
      Given "nmap" is installed
      And the following profile:
        | name      | value                  |
        | host      | nodegoat.kerokuapp.com |


    Scenario: Verify the security header using the http-security-headers
      When I launch a "nmap" attack with:
        """
        nmap -p80 --script http-security-headers <host>
        """
      Then the output should contain "X-Frame-Options: DENY"
```

Summary

This chapter summarizes some of key security automation tips and techniques.

In the automation testing framework, we compared the common UI automation frameworks, such as Macaca, AutoIT, Selenium, Appium, and Sikuli. We demonstrated most of the cases in Selenium in this book. For BDD frameworks, there is Robot Framework, Behave, Jgiven, and Gauntlt. Robot Framework and Gauntlt are mostly illustrated with case studies in the previous chapters.

For secure code review, we listed the code patterns that related to common security issues, such as insecure protocol, weak encryption, and hard-coded information. Some source code search tools are also introduced, such as GREP rough Audit and GrepBugs.

For API security testing, the testing tools, ZAP, JMeter, FuzzDB, and ZAP OpenAPI are demonstrated. We also discussed some sources of FuzzDB and how to generate your custom security payloads for testing. In addition, the techniques of Fuzz Testing are also demonstrated by using ZAP, JMeter, Selenium DTT, Robot Framework DDT, 0d1n, and Wfuzz.

As regards web security testing, we introduced how to automate the web scanner, ZAP, by using ZAP-CLI and RESTful API. The common security scan operations are Spider scan, active scan, and generate a report.

For Android security testing, we introduced some tools to do secure code scan, privacy scan, reverse engineering, and automated security scan. We also introduced the white box review tips, secure code patterns, and risky APIs.

For the infrastructure security, there are three key areas: known vulnerable components scan, secure configuration inspection, and secure communication. We introduced the tools for these security inspections. In addition, we also demonstrated the uses of Nmap for various kinds of security scanning.

For the BDD security testing, we introduced how to automate the ZAP Spider scan in Robot Framework. We also demonstrated the uses of Robot Framework to sign in the NodeGoat with SQL injection security payloads. The Nmap and SQLmap security scans are also demonstrated by using Robot Framework. Besides, we also demonstrated the uses of another BDD security testing framework, Gauntlt, for the Nmap scan.

We learned how to implement automation security in all layers of software frameworks and also how to build an in-house security automation platform throughout software releases.

List of Scripts and Tools

You may get related demo scripts from the GitHub link: `https://github.com/PacktPublishing/Practical-Security-Automation-and-Testing`. In addition, there is a Virtual Box Ubuntu installed with all the tools mentioned in this book. The credentials of the Ubuntu are listed here:

- Username: `osbox`
- Password: `osbox.org`

List of sample scripts

The following table gives the description of files/scripts used:

Name of files/scripts	Description
`nmap_NodeGoat.robot`	This demonstrates how to apply Robot Framework with NMAP.
`nmap_NodeGoat_gauntlt.attack`	This is the BDD framework Gauntlt testing script that defines NMAP scan against NodeGoat.
`NodeGoat_SignIn.py`	Selenium Python script to do the sign-in of the NodeGoat website.
`NodeGoat.jmx`	JMeter data-driven testing to sign in the NodeGoat website with the `sqli.csv` payloads.
`MyRequest.jmx`	JMeter data-driven testing to sign in the `demo.testfire.net` with the `sqli.csv` payloads.
`RF_DDT.robot`	Robot Framework data-driven testing to sign in to the NodeGoat with the `sqli.csv` payloads.
`Selenium Proxy Sample.py`	Selenium Python script to demonstrate how to define proxy in the browser profile.
`SignIn_DDT.py`	Selenium Python data-driven testing scrip to sign in testfire with `sqli.csv` data.
`SignIn_DDT_NodeGoat.py`	Selenium Python data-driven testing scrip to sign in to NodeGoat with `sqli.csv` data.
`sqli.csv` `cmdi.csv`	Sample security data payloads from the FuzzDB.
`UserRegistration.py`	The Selenium Python script demonstrates user registration with predefined data on the website: `http://hackazon.webscantest.com/`.

List of installed tools in virtual image

The password of the `root` is `osboxes.org`. Here are some of the tools installed in the VM and their usage:

Installed Tools	Description and Usage
`NodeGoat`	Vulnerable source code of NodeGoat project.
`0d1n`	This is used for fuzz testing. Use the keyword ^ for the fuzz testing data. `$ ./0d1n`
`androwarn`	It's a static code analyzer for malicious Android applications. `$ python androwarn.py --help`

`archerysec`	This is an Open Source Vulnerability Assessment and Management that helps developers and pentesters perform scans and manage vulnerabilities.
	`$ docker pull archerysec/archerysec`
	`$ docker run -it -p 8000:8000 archerysec/archerysec:latest`

`qark`	This is a Python tool to look for several security-related Android application vulnerabilities. `$python qarkMain.py`
`radamsa`	This is a dynamic fuzz data generator. `$echo "Sample Data"	radamsa`
`RetireJS`	This scans the JavaScript libraries for known vulnerable components. `$ retire`
`gauntlt`	This is the BDD security testing framework. `$ gauntlt`
`DumpsterDiver`	This searches the password, key, or hash by using entropy values. `$ python DumpsterDiver.py`
`robotframework`	This is an acceptance testing framework. `$ robot --help`
`sslscan`	This is used to inspect the secure configurations of the SSL. `$ sslscan`
`wfuzz`	This is a web fuzz testing tool. Use the keyword FUZZ to apply the fuzz testing data. `$ wfuzz -w xss.csv --hc 404 http://<target_host>/FUZZ`
`zap-cli`	This can operate and automate the ZAP scanning under CLI mode. `$ zap-cli --help`

`vulscan`	This scans known vulnerabilities. `$ nmap --script vulscan.nse <host>`
`grep-it.sh`	This searches for security issues in source code by using GREP. `$ grep-it.sh`
`goatdroid.apk` `InsecureBankv2.apk`	These are Vulnerable APKs, which we demonstrated in case studies.

`Mobile Security Framework`	This is Mobile
	`$docker pull opensecurity/mobile-security-framework-mobsf`
	`$docker run -it -p 8000:8000 opensecurity/mobile-security-framework-mobsf:latest`
	Launch browser with `http://127.0.0.1:8000/` to access the MobSF Web interface.

`ZAP`	OWASP ZAP Web security scanner. `$ owasp-zap`
`NMAP`	Network security scanner. `$ namp`
`DejectDojo`	OWASP DejectDojo To manage testing findings and reports. `$ docker run -it -p 8000:8000 appsecpipeline/django-defectdojo bash -c "export LOAD_SAMPLE_DATA=True && bash /opt/django-DefectDojo/docker/docker-startup.bash"`
`RapidScan`	Python script to execute several security testing tools. `$ python rapidscan.py`

Solutions

Chapter 1: The Scope and Challenges of Security Automation

Questions	Answers
Q1	2
Q2	3
Q3	3
Q4	1
Q5	3

Chapter 2: Integrating Security and Automation

Questions	Answers
Q1	1
Q2	4
Q3	4
Q4	3
Q5	4

Chapter 3: Secure Code Inspection

Questions	Answers
Q1	1
Q2	4
Q3	4
Q4	1
Q5	4

Chapter 4: Sensitive Information and Privacy Testing

Questions	Answers
Q1	1
Q2	4
Q3	3
Q4	1

Chapter 5: Security API and Fuzz Testing

Questions	Answers
Q1	3
Q2	4
Q3	4
Q4	1
Q5	1

Chapter 6: Web Application Security Testing

Questions	Answers
Q1	1
Q2	4
Q3	3
Q4	3

Chapter 7: Android Security Testing

Questions	Answers
Q1	4
Q2	2
Q3	4
Q4	3
Q5	3

Chapter 8: Infrastructure Security

Questions	Answers
Q1	4
Q2	3
Q3	1
Q4	4
Q5	4
Q6	3

Chapter 9: BDD Acceptance Security Testing

Questions	Answers
Q1	4
Q2	4
Q3	2
Q4	2
Q5	2

Chapter 10: Project Background and Automation Approach

Questions	Answers
Q1	4
Q2	4
Q3	1
Q4	4
Q5	4

Chapter 11: Automated Testing for Web Applications

Questions	Answers
Q1	4
Q2	1
Q3	1
Q4	4
Q5	4

Chapter 12: Automated Fuzz API Security Testing

Questions	Answers
Q1	4
Q2	3
Q3	1
Q4	3
Q5	3

Chapter 13: Automated Infrastructure Security

Questions	Answers
Q1	1
Q2	1
Q3	4
Q4	4
Q5	4

Chapter 14: Managing and Presenting Test Results

Questions	Answers
Q1	4
Q2	1
Q3	2
Q4	4
Q5	4

Other Books You May Enjoy

If you enjoyed this book, you may be interested in these other books by Packt:

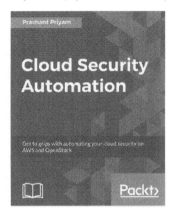

Cloud Security Automation
Prashant Priyam

ISBN: 978-1-78862-786-3

- Define security for public and private cloud services
- Address the security concerns of your cloud
- Understand Identity and Access Management
- Get acquainted with cloud storage and network security
- Improve and optimize public and private cloud security
- Automate cloud security
- Understand the security compliance requirements of your cloud

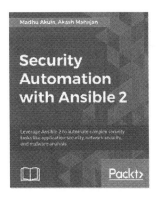

Security Automation with Ansible 2
Madhu Akula, Akash Mahajan

ISBN: 978-1-78839-451-2

- Use Ansible playbooks, roles, modules, and templating to build generic, testable playbooks
- Manage Linux and Windows hosts remotely in a repeatable and predictable manner
- See how to perform security patch management, and security hardening with scheduling and automation
- Set up AWS Lambda for a serverless automated defense
- Run continuous security scans against your hosts and automatically fix and harden the gaps
- Extend Ansible to write your custom modules and use them as part of your already existing security automation programs
- Perform automation security audit checks for applications using Ansible
- Manage secrets in Ansible using Ansible Vault

Leave a review - let other readers know what you think

Please share your thoughts on this book with others by leaving a review on the site that you bought it from. If you purchased the book from Amazon, please leave us an honest review on this book's Amazon page. This is vital so that other potential readers can see and use your unbiased opinion to make purchasing decisions, we can understand what our customers think about our products, and our authors can see your feedback on the title that they have worked with Packt to create. It will only take a few minutes of your time, but is valuable to other potential customers, our authors, and Packt. Thank you!

Index

Printed in Great Britain
by Amazon